MOTIVATIONAL LEADERSHIP

Also by Alfred Tack

MARKETING AND MANAGEMENT BOOKS

Executive Development
Building, Training, and Motivating a Sales Force
How to Overcome Nervous Tension and Speak Well in Public
How to Double Your Income in Selling
1000 Ways to Increase your Sales
Sell Better – Live Better
Sell Your Way to Success
How to Train Yourself to Succeed in Selling
How to Increase Sales by Telephone
Profitable Letter Writing
How to Increase Your Sales to Industry
How to Succeed in Selling
How to Sell Successfully Overseas
Professional Salesmanship
Successful Sales Management
Marketing, The Sales Manager's Role
How to Succeed as a Sales Manager

FICTION

The Great Hijack
The Spy Who wasn't Exchanged
The Top Steal
Forecast – Murder
Murder Takes Over
P A to Murder
Death Kicks a Pebble
Selling's Murder
Interviewing's Killing
The Prospect's Dead
The Test Match Murder
A Murder is Staged
Killing Business
Death Takes a Dive
Return of the Assassin

Motivational Leadership

Alfred Tack

WILDWOOD HOUSE

This paperback edition published 1986 by
Wildwood House Limited,
Gower House,
Croft Road,
Aldershot,
Hampshire GU11 3HR,
England

Reprinted 1989

British Library Cataloguing in Publication Data

Tack, Alfred
   Motivational leadership.
   1. Employee motivation   2. Personnel
   management   3. Leadership
   I. Title
   658.3'14   HF5549.5.M63

   ISBN 0-7045-0548-7

Typeset in Great Britain
by Graphic Studios (Southern) Ltd, Godalming, Surrey.

Printed and bound in Great Britain at
The Camelot Press plc, Southampton

Contents

Foreword

by Nigel Farrow, Managing Director, Gower Publishing
Company Ltd

This is a unique book, written by a unique person.
Alfred Tack is co-chairman and managing director of a
highly diversified industrial group of companies.

Year after year, Tack Industries Ltd has consistently
and profitably grown into one of the most successful
organisations of its kind in the country. Possibly the best
known of the companies is Tack Training International
Ltd, which is a large, international training company
providing courses in forty-five countries.

But there is another side to Alfred Tack. He is a
prolific author, having had seventeen books on management, marketing, communication and salesmanship published – all bestsellers in their field – and fifteen thriller/
novels, two of which have been filmed and one serialised
on BBC radio.

Tack has now combined all his talents as an industrial-
ist, management consultant, trainer and author by
writing a most original book. *Motivational Leadership*
reads like a popular novel, teaches motivational leadership in a series of workshops, and continually involves
the reader in the decision making process.

It tells the story of how Don McAllister, a leading US
management consultant, investigates the leadership
qualities of a large British industrial group. The assignment has two objectives: the first is to improve leadership
qualities – with the emphasis on motivating to improve
managerial performance; the second, to find a successor

to the chief executive, Roland Huntley, who has announced his intention of retiring.

The philosophy of motivational leadership is summed up by the marketing director, Tom Lawson, who says:

> "A leader can be a fine strategist, an innovator, have a good financial brain . . . but whatever his objectives, he has to get others to see them through. There may be those who are all bright-eyed and bushy-tailed, ready to implement these objectives with drive, accuracy, and enthusiasm, but the majority do need to be motivated continually, to give of their best – and the chief executive should be the chief motivator . . ."

The reader may become so involved with the directors and their relationships with each other – the jockeying for position – that some of the well researched lessons taught in each chapter will be overlooked: Possibly the greatest benefit will be derived from the book by first reading it right through from beginning to end to enjoy the interplay of people and ideas, and then following this by a more careful study of relevant chapters.

This book is for all those in management – whether main board directors or middle managers – who are concerned with the effectiveness of their leadership.

1 An Assignment for McAllister

The formalities had been completed, the proposal from McAllister & Associates accepted by Roland Huntley and his directors.

Huntley, in his boardroom, sitting in a leather high-backed chair, reflected on the past, and once more considered the future.

At sixty-three he gave himself two more years as chief executive of the Huntley Group. He thought too objectively to believe that at seventy he would still be the driving force his company needed. Soon, he would have to nominate a successor.

Huntley's were the largest European group of companies in the fire fighting field, marketing appliances ranging from small fire extinguishers to completely fitted tenders, sold to fire brigades throughout the world.

Roland Huntley had built the company from modest beginnings, and it had prospered year after year, until the recession. Then came a 'mark time' period. It is an old tag that only efficient companies call in consultants before it is too late, and the Huntley Group were highly efficient. Huntley blamed himself, mostly, for the cessation of corporate growth, because during all previous recessions the group had increased profits. His board of directors had insisted that to be able to mark time during the recession was a minor triumph, and that no one was to blame. Huntley could not accept this argument. He believed that his colleagues on the board had become too complacent, and was both surprised and pleased that they had so readily agreed to call in consultants to check every aspect of the group's activities. Possibly each thought that such an investigation would find weaknesses in his colleagues' departments, while there would be only praise for his own.

McAllister's were the obvious choice. Not only were they respected world-wide as a consultancy group, but he had known their founder, Hugh McAllister, for many years. McAllister's were leaders because while the majority of consultancy organisations employed a small number of brilliant men and a great number of very average consultants, McAllister's only employed brilliant, highly-paid men and women. Most of them, in fact, could carry out their own proposals – something few consultants could do.

Roland Huntley's first objective in calling in McAllister was to discover whether, in fact, his group were doing very well by marking time or, as he believed, they had slipped backwards. His second objective, he kept from the board. He needed another opinion as to which of his directors should succeed him as chief executive.

Roland contemplated the boardroom, which was so changed, on the instigation of his co-directors, from its original concept twenty years earlier. Then, it had been all polished mahogany and nineteenth-century paintings. Now, it was modern in concept, having been designed by Mateo of Italy, and the paintings – lines, blobs, triangles – were all very colourful. He had, however, insisted on retaining his leather high-backed chair.

A few minutes before the appointed time, Tom Lawson, the marketing director, arrived. Aged forty-two, he had joined the company as a salesman and had risen via area manager, management, sales management, to regional director, and thence to main board marketing director.

Following him came financial director, Lawrence Duckworth, who had joined the company at the age of thirty, and had been financial director for ten years. He was now forty-five.

The production director and the director of personnel arrived together. Bill Manley, forty-nine, had only been with the company six years. He had been engaged as works director at the Dorset plant, and had been so successful in reducing costs that after his third year he was invited to join the main board.

The personnel director, Hugh Fairley, at thirty-eight, had a good record in personnel, and had been head hunted for Roland seven years earlier.

The men stood about and talked of recent developments, until Don McAllister was ushered in by Roland's secretary.

Don McAllister, at forty, the son of the founder of the consultancy group, was president of the European organisation. Tall, slim, tanned complexion, clear blue eyes – he could have been the prototype for all USA executives.

Roland escorted him to his chair, and returned to his own seat, wasting no more time on pleasantries.

"Don is here," he began, "because he wants to talk to us collectively, although we have all agreed to the McAllister proposal, which covers . . ."

Marketing director Lawson glanced at financial director Duckworth; they read each other's thoughts. Roland was always preaching brevity in communication, but at most board meetings he would repeat – and repeat again – facts already known to all of them, and fully discussed. Roland continued blithely with his summary: "Don has told us that the majority of chief executives believe they know where weaknesses lie – lack of direction, weak marketing, poor corporate strategy, no financial control . . . But we don't know; we can't pinpoint any specific weakness, we believe we are efficient in every sphere of activity. But in spite of this, our profits have not increased in line with our previous performances. Possibly he will conclude that we are not making any major errors, but that there has been an accumulation of minor problems which should not have occurred. For example, do our directors still walk the shop floors to try to foresee and forestall problems? . . ."

Please stop, thought Lawson, *I have an afternoon appointment, and there is no need to make a speech to impress Don McAllister*. But still Huntley continued, emphasising the enormous cost of employing McAllister's organisation and, therefore, the need for close co-operation by all the directors.

Bill Manley, stocky, overweight, with a belt drawn tightly emphasising his overhanging stomach, began to feel drowsy, but pulled himself together when he heard Roland Huntley saying, "Well, that's all from me. Now it's up to you, Don."

McAllister opened his black leather brief case, removed a sheaf of papers, and laid them neatly in front of him. He began talking in his soft but resonant voice: "Gentlemen, from the cursory examination we have been able to make so far I do not think we are going to find very much radically wrong with the Huntley Group. You are an efficient organisation. Firstly, I want to give you details of the members of each team that will be assigned to the various areas . . ." He continued to read out a list of names of his consultants, giving full background and experience of each of them. He handed printed details to each of the directors, giving them just enough time to glance at the sheet of paper before going on, "As you know, our first step is always to appraise all of the employees – not just the management team – and to explain to them how we work and why you have called us in, and that our objective is to help create greater expansion, resulting in greater job security."

"I agree with that approach," interrupted Huntley, "and must tell you that I have used it myself on many occasions. Unfortunately, it has dropped by the wayside. Now we talk mostly to the managers, and the managers pass on the messages down the line. Who will undertake the task of addressing our staff?"

"I shall," said McAllister. "And then no one else can be blamed if our consultants come up against an anti-consultant lobby, either among the managers or the work force generally. In case you are at all concerned, because you obviously have militants in your organisation who will disagree with everything management does, I can assure you that with every assignment we have undertaken so far, our approach has always worked well. Incidentally, we make a point of discussing the militants' problems with them, directly. After these meetings we have further discussions with the regional directors and their managers, where we spell out to them our exact objectives. Usually, we are not very warmly received by management. To them, it always appears a time-wasting experience. It is essential that we talk quickly to the majority of employees, because there are always leaks, and once a leak occurs there is wonder, concern, fear – and it is much more difficult then to eradicate impressions already formed than it is to impress those whose minds are not closed."

McAllister continued explaining procedure for some twenty minutes, then, for the first time, he smiled. Looking at each director in turn he said, "It's obvious that all the main board directors work very long hours and have little spare time, yet I am now going to ask you to find time for a series of quite lengthy meetings."

The executive team eyed McAllister warily as he continued "I appreciate that in spite of the recession you still made high profits by whatever ratio we accept – profit against working capital, against turnover, per employee . . . There can be few companies who have enjoyed such successes as you have achieved during the past years. It is true you haven't shown substantial increases in profits during this period, but that's why you have sought our help – or perhaps advice would be a better word. Yet you all believe that something must be wrong, because with your expertise, brilliant management, innovative record, profit should continually increase substantially. As Roland has emphasised, fires occur in every country whatever the economic climate, and in most countries, fire protection is obligatory. We have found – and I need hardly remind you that our experience is world-wide – that when such setbacks occur in companies like yours, it is rarely due completely to one or more of the basic faults. This was put most succinctly by Roger Hurn, managing director of Smiths Industries, and chairman of the BIM panel dealing with 'Improving Management Performance'. He stated that there is rarely any need for some new theory or technique to be adopted to improve performance. What is required is the determination and application of relatively few principles of planning, personnel relationships, and leadership, to be applied at all levels."

McAllister paused for effect, then went on, "We have found that marking time by companies that have had many years of success can often be due to a failure of leadership, and it applies right down the line. Possibly the most important aspect of this assignment is to analyse the leadership factor."

The atmosphere, so far friendly, changed instantly, as Don knew it would. Each director was prepared to admit that there could always be technical improvements, but bad leadership? That was ridiculous!

Don said gently, "Now you're annoyed with me – it always happens. I am no longer the blue-eyed boy from the USA, here to find out the misdeeds of the others." There was a quality in his voice which eased the tension.

Roland Huntley eased it even more by saying, "You

may well be right, Don, but are you referring to me, the board, or the divisional managers?"

"At this stage, Roland, I am not referring to anyone. I am only stating a fact which we, from our extensive experience, have gleaned. It is almost axiomatic that after years of success the value of good leadership is often forgotten, and the value of good management extolled. That surprises you? I'll explain my views later, but there is one point I want to make: it is that leadership and motivation are synonymous. If, in a well run company, the leadership is no longer so dynamic as once it was, it is possible that motivational forces have weakened, resulting in less production, fewer sales, less innovation. And few would notice or recognise what has happened, because no one would appear to be directly affected. After many years a chief executive can become a paternalistic leader rather than an all-round effective leader. Roland, please remember I am still giving facts from past cases. So far, we have not yet considered whether or not it applies to Huntley's – but if there is a leadership weakness, it goes right down the line. It applies just as much to the R & D division as to the sales teams. In each, the effect is slight but cumulatively it has a strong effect on profitability."

McAllister paused for comments, and Roland said immediately, "You need not continue, Don, you've made a valid point. Possibly I no longer inspire others as I should do."

From the directors came a chorus of denials – "No, no!" – "Of course not!" – "That isn't the case!" . . .

Huntley shook his head. "Let us face facts: if I have not given you effective leadership and you, in turn, have not led others as they should be led, that could be our problem."

"Our years of success," he added, "have probably made us believe that we have such a great team spirit that everyone pulls his weight, without strong motivation, but how are you going to find out whether this is a weakness or not? I doubt whether anyone will tell you."

"Of course they won't," answered McAllister. "You will have to discover it for yourselves. You are all working flat out – I've had trouble trying to tie some of you down for even a fifteen minute discussion – and you've told me how your diaries are all booked, for weeks ahead; yet I'm going to ask you to cancel some of those appointments. I know all of them are important – they always are – but if you think the assignment you have given us is the more important, then I ask you to get together and find a series of dates for meetings.

"These will take the form of workshops, where we can throw the ball at each other and, at the end, possibly find a solution to leadership problems, if they 'exist. Once these have been completed, similar meetings will have to be arranged between you and your managers, then by our managers . . . right down the line to shop supervisors. You already are highly successful leaders, but can there still be improvements? It is for you to decide." He looked around for some response.

Huntley said, "Your plan must be put into practice. It is no use employing consultants and then refusing to co-operate. Time must be found. I shall attend each session personally."

Don shook his head. "No, Roland, if you don't mind! That would be an inhibiting factor. I should be grateful if you would attend the final session when I hope we shall have come to a definite conclusion."

"What shape will these sessions take?" asked Lawson.

"We shall sit around a table – or we needn't even have a table. And the meetings can take place anywhere. Before each of them, I shall indicate to you the aspect of leadership that we are going to discuss. Before we even consider leadership in any depth we shall have to highlight some of the ingredients. We already know that the leader must be a motivator, but he must also be a decision maker, a problem solver, a negotiator . . . But here again, I must ask: have I your co-operation? And this is not a decision which can be made for you by Roland!"

"You have mine, most decidedly," said Tom Lawson. "You're right, the whole marketing field could be improved, right across the board – not by new ideas, but by better leadership, to get the best out of those we employ."

Larry Duckworth said, "With reservations – yes. Although at this stage I can't see how finance and leadership are tied up."

"That applies to me, too," said Bill Manley. "It'll be interesting to discuss new ways of motivating militant trade union shop stewards."

Hugh Fairley declared that he was one hundred per cent in agreement, emphasising that personnel management and leadership were also synonymous.

Roland Huntley said briefly, "Well, gentlemen, that ends this meeting. Do, please, make the necessary arrangements with Don as soon as possible, and let me have the dates." Then turning to McAllister he said, "Please stay, Don. I want to discuss another matter with you."

As the directors trooped out they all knew that the 'other matter' could only be themselves.

When the door closed behind them Huntley moved away from the top of the table and sat alongside McAllister. "Don," he said, "you did a grand job; but the hard part is to come. I didn't want there to be any discussion at this stage, that's why I closed the meeting after they had agreed to the meetings."

"You're not sure whether I have won them over?"

"I don't think that was possible, at this stage. They are top class executives, and each one of them thinks he has forgotten more about leadership than you will ever know. They agreed with your request because they had no alternative. Frankly, I don't believe there is much wrong with my leadership."

"Well, you know," said McAllister, stroking his chin thoughtfully, "all entrepreneurs are the same."

"How do you mean?"

"They tend to treat even their most highly paid executives as schoolchildren and that, Roland, is not really very good leadership."

Huntley looked puzzled. "Are you suggesting that this applies to me, too?"

"On the face of it, yes. When the meeting began you almost barked at us to attend – as if you were a sergeant major and we were new recruits. During the meeting they were all looking at you for guidance. And at the end there was almost a peremptory demand on your part for them to go. They all trooped out again, like schoolchildren, instructed to disappear by their headmaster."

For a moment Huntley looked angry. Then he pursed his lips. Finally, his face broke into a broad smile, which illuminated it with warmth and understanding.

"And that," he said, "is, no doubt, your first lesson in leadership."

2 Leadership Priorities

The first meeting of the committee was held at the Berkeley Hotel, adjacent to Hyde Park.

McAllister had explained to Roland Huntley that a relaxed atmosphere was essential during the sparring phase, to avoid a fighting situation later. He knew that without the presence of the chief executive, there would be tension, coolness and status seeking, at the initial meeting.

McAllister decided to stay at the Berkeley overnight, and to invite the directors to join him for breakfast. That, he thought, would make common ground for all four directors: they could discuss the idiosyncrasies of the Americans before the meeting began. Most British executives, he knew, believed that breakfast time was sacrosanct – an occasion for reading the newspapers, ignoring the children, and eating bacon and eggs; certainly not the time for innovation, or problem solving.

Having read their thoughts correctly, McAllister suggested on their arrival that they all have a pre-breakfast swim in the roof garden pool. An obliging pool attendant supplied the swimming trunks, and much to their surprise the main board of Huntley's thoroughly enjoyed the early morning swim. Suddenly, the nonsense of a breakfast meeting in McAllister's sitting-room seemed rather a good idea, and it was jokingly suggested that they now put forward a new health policy for Huntley's, and install a swimming pool at headquarters.

Over breakfast, McAllister regaled them with brief stories of time spent in Hong Kong, Malaysia, Japan, and other parts of the world, and the directors, all equally keen not to be outdone, tried to cap his stories – and they met with success because McAllister was an ardent listener.

The breakfast table cleared, McAllister began the meeting. "First," he said, "please feel free to air your objections, because unless I can allay your suspicions that this is a consultant's ploy to justify high fees or that you have been invited to listen to academic theories on leadership, this meeting won't make much progress. Briefly, then, what were your criticisms following our last meeting? What did you discuss with each other? What did you tell your families? Tom, you make a start."

"You've hit the nail right on the head," said Tom, "I can tell you now what we all thought – possibly, what some of us still think: you are an academic with, as I understand it, little experience of business leadership, so all we expect to get is a rehash of Maslow, Herzberg, McGregor, Humble, and the rest. We, at Huntley's, are a little tired of the research of some professors with conclusions which were already obvious to any businessman worth his salt. It's all good stuff for the would-be executives and graduates, but not for us. How about that for starters, Don?"

"Fair comment! I'd have made the same in your position. Now your turn, Larry."

"As financial director I don't lead anyone – except, possibly, the Inland Revenue up the garden path sometimes."

McAllister smiled at the weak humour, and nodded towards the personnel director, Hugh Fairley.

Hugh said, "Well, I'm not criticising you. We run a number of in-house leadership courses and I have sent some of our managers to outside courses, too. Some have benefited, some have not; but we can discuss the reasons later."

"And you, Bill?" McAllister expected a no-nonsense reply from the production director, Bill Manley, and he got it. Although he was running to fat, Bill Manley still looked as tough as he was.

"Lead by example," he said, "that's what I say."

McAllister paused for a moment, then said, "Now I'll try to answer your criticisms. Firstly, I hardly think you can call me an academic. It's true that I am a graduate of the Harvard Business School, but no one has ever been condemned for attending that academy of business studies. On leaving there I spent my first three years with IBM, then two years as managing director of a relatively small company employing some six hundred people manufacturing and marketing room coolers. Only after that experience, which is, I think, fairly substantial, did my father bring me into the McAllister Group. Then I had a further two years of consultancy training before taking over my first assignment. Now I control a European team of over three hundred consultants. That needs leadership! Have I made my point?"

"Very well indeed," said Tom Lawson.

"Would it be fair," continued McAllister, "to ask you to look on me as a coach – although as top executives of a large company, you don't feel you need coaching? But perhaps there's an analogy with sport. Let me give you an example. Probably one of the greatest golfers of all time is Jack Nicklaus. In a series of articles he wrote recently he tells how he spends more and more time with his coach because, as he maintains, you often can't see your own faults. To quote his words: 'What I request of Grout – the professional coach – is a full review of fundamentals.' Don't you think we can equate the views of Nicklaus with our present situation?"

"That's a very good analogy," said Tom Lawson. "O.K. I'm prepared to be coached."

Even Bill Manley had to agree that there might be

something in reviewing fundamentals, although he couldn't quite credit that he could be doing anything wrong.

"You're so right, Bill," said McAllister. "But being human beings it is very difficult for us to see our own faults, although we can always readily see the faults in others. I don't think that during these discussions we are going to learn a lot that's new; but perhaps we can remind ourselves of practices and principles long forgotten."

"You've made your point," said Hugh Fairley. "You've read our minds correctly and answered our criticisms; so now let's get on with our meeting."

McAllister said, "Right! Then let me first answer Larry's query. He doesn't believe that leadership applies to him. How many staff do you employ directly, Larry?"

"Directly," Duckworth mused, "with the computer division and various accounts departments, about fifty directly, and many more indirectly."

"Under your control you have several managers?"

"Well, they're accountants."

"But they are managers – they manage divisions?"

"Yes."

"And do they always give one hundred per cent effort to their jobs?"

"No one does that!"

"But that should be their objective, shouldn't it?"

"Yes."

"So do you agree with me that bad leadership would have an adverse effect on your managers?"

"Of course!"

"Then you must also agree that anything better than 'bad' right up to one hundred per cent brilliant must have a positive effect."

"Very clever," said Larry. "You've done this particular exercise many times – you've thought it all out so well. I don't fully agree with you, but I'll go along, for the time being."

McAllister turned to Bill Manley. "And you said you lead by example, Bill. I'm sure you set the right example, but what about your regional works directors and works managers, their foremen and supervisors? Do they always set the right example? Could they copy your style of leadership which, I know, is a very tough, almost autocratic style? Can we improve their leadership qualities?"

"Yes," said Bill, who was quite happy to agree that others could be improved, so long as he, personally, was not under attack.

"O.K.," said McAllister. "Now let me throw out a question for discussion: is good leadership synonymous with good management?"

"Most definitely," said Bill Manley.

Larry Duckworth inhaled cigarette smoke deeply, much to the disgust of Fairley, a non-smoker, and said, "Again, I can only partly agree. I don't consider myself a natural leader – that is, if I'm a leader at all – but I do believe that I'm an effective manager."

Tom Lawson, immaculate in blue suit, blue striped shirt with white collar, and polka dot tie, said, "They aren't synonymous at all. A good leader need not necessarily be a good manager. Often, the manager carries out the dictates of the leader. That's how it is at the highest levels. At lower levels the shop steward may have to be a manager as well as a leader. If, however, he is a good leader, he will often get better results than if he is only a good manager."

"I can't see that," interrupted Bill Manley. "I believe I'm a good manager – and no snide remarks, if you please. And I have good managers under me. I think part of good management is, undoubtedly, good leadership."

"No, you're wrong," said Lawson. "My function as marketing director is no different from yours as production director. You control three factories in this country; two of them have works directors, and you, yourself, are mostly in control of our largest plant in Dorset. My job as marketing director is not only concerned with pricing, advertising, sales promotion, and negotiating – my main job is to motivate the sales directors and sales managers, so that they, in turn, can motivate the field sales managers, area managers, and salesmen. What do you do, Bill, when there's an outcry for greater production?"

"I begin by fighting the unions," grunted Manley.

"Come off it, Bill, that rarely happens – and you know it! First you consider ways and means of increasing production, and you have to implement them with consultations. Maybe that's not your style – but you know it's going to lead to problems if you don't have consultations. And when you have consultations you have to motivate others. That's what all good leaders do. You motivate people – and so do I."

Manley shrugged his shoulders. "I still believe that, mainly, I'm a manager."

"And I believe," said Lawson, "that you are mainly a leader, and that the management function is carried out by others."

"O.K.," said Manley, "then tell me the difference between a manager and a leader – other than your motivational theory."

"I'll let Don do that!" finished Lawson. McAllister did not take up the challenge.

"You know, Bill's right, as usual," said Larry Duckworth, winking at Tom Lawson.

"I don't want any of your sarcasm, Larry," said Bill, "but I agree, I always *am* right."

"I must say I agree to some extent with Bill," said Larry. "If a department is not well managed no amount of leadership will stop the chaos, with all the attendant problems of mismanagement."

"You're going to extremes, as usual," said Lawson.

"Let's get back to fundamentals. Why are we here? The Old Man is concerned that if we don't take action now, we could be on the slide. What he wants to know is why management has failed. Don, here, feels that if it has failed it is due to bad leadership on our part, and on the part of other executives."

"I have a simple mind," said Bill Manley, believing no such thing, "and I like simple explanations. No one has given me the answer. I believe good management and good leadership are one and the same thing."

Don McAllister had been sitting back, thoroughly enjoying the debate. Everything had gone as expected. *Get four intelligent businessmen together,* he thought, *and each will show strength; each will believe he is right; but eventually, because they are good executives, they will be open to reason – and being open to reason, will revise their own thinking, if necessary.* He thought the time had now arrived for him to take a hand. "May I come in now," he said, "and deal with your query, Bill?"

"Are you still with us?" asked Hugh Fairley. "We thought you'd gone home." The ensuing laughter relaxed the situation.

"Let us take as an example," said McAllister, "the manager of a dairy depot. His sole job is to make sure that supplies arrive on time, that the milkmen are punctual, and deliveries can be maintained to local householders. He insists on the milk floats being kept clean, and inspects them whenever he has the time. However, if things go wrong and the milkmen don't keep their floats as clean as they should, or the deliveries don't arrive on time, he blames top management. They have not replaced old floats as they should have or they are not tough enough with suppliers . . . But most of all he blames them for underpaying him and the milkmen with whom he identifies. He ensures that the takings match the sales, and if the milkmen make a little on the side, so what? He is a manager, he does a reasonable job. But in no way is he a leader, because he makes no attempt to motivate others. Admittedly, in an ideal business world all managers would be leaders – that is our objective for the Huntley Group.

"Let us take another example – and this is a true one, but as we were the consultants involved I'd better change the names and venues. Stephen Lock was the manager in charge of a large store – part of a well-known chain. He considered himself to be a leader and a manager. He was punctilious in everything he did. To enhance the store's image he took part in local affairs and was on several committees. Lock kept a tight rein, checking management accounts, line by line. He had installed a highly efficient system for cutting down pilfering by employees, which involved a great deal of work for the computers and much form filling. He had given strict instructions to his supervisors that they must check the displays every morning and check the appearance of the staff. He was in close touch with the buying situation, so he considered himself to be a first-class manager and leader. But the store's turnover had not increased – in fact, it was decreasing, which is one of the reasons we were called in.

"Lock walked round the store once a day smiling, pointing out minor faults – but it was a very fast walk-around, because he hadn't much time to spare. However, we discovered that from a customer's point of view, too many of the staff were ill-mannered and surly, and lacked interest in the work they were doing. The supervisors, while bowing low before their chief, tended to side with the staff, and if there were any complaints it was always the customer's fault. So, you see, Stephen Lock was a manager doing all the things a good manager should do to maintain control, but he was not a leader – he did not motivate anyone to achieve better results which, in most cases, means satisfying customer needs. At the other extreme we have Roland Huntley who is a leader, but not a manager."

Hugh Fairley interrupted, "Shouldn't we first define leadership then, Don, and what it entails?"

Everyone agreed but McAllister said, "I'd rather leave that till later, Hugh. In fact we may find that the essential attributes of a leader may only emerge from time to time at our meetings, and we shan't reach any conclusion until our final meeting."

"I'd like to say this," said Tom Lawson. "A leader can be a fine strategist, an innovator, have a good financial brain . . . But whatever his objectives, strategies, new concepts, he has to get others to see them through. There may be others who are all bright-eyed and bushy-tailed, ready to implement these objectives with drive, accuracy, and enthusiasm, but the majority do need motivating – especially as, these days, we all believe we are underpaid."

"You're right, Tom," said Fairley. "The average Mr & Mrs no longer want to keep up with the Jones's, they want to keep up with Sheik Jones or Lord Jones – and who can blame them? We all want something better. The question is how to achieve it? Don says, by motivating others, but if you want to put it to the vote right now I'm quite sure we all agree that the prime function of a leader is to motivate."

"And," said Tom Lawson, "the chief executive should be the chief motivator."

"That's right," said Don, "which brings us to the objective of this meeting: do we – and by we I mean myself included because I, too, have a team to look after – motivate others as we should? Obviously, our next meeting should be devoted solely to motivation. But let me stress our objective: I have given examples of managers who failed to motivate their employees to achieve higher performances. From my experience, possibly eight per cent of managers are not leaders and, therefore, fail to get the best out of their staff. This must result in some form of loss to their companies. If the local dairy manager was not a leader – who was to blame? If the store director was a poor leader – again, who was to blame? Obviously, it was the dairy manager's superior, and the store director's managing director. Managers too often manage departments, manage people – but do not lead them.

"Very few employees work to their true potential. Effective leadership motivates them *willingly* – and that is the operative word – to stretch their minds and physical attributes to greater purpose.

"It is our objective to improve the leadership qualities of every manager in the Huntley Group, and I admire you all for agreeing to review all the leadership fundamentals."

He paused. No one made any comment, so changing from his previous forceful tones McAllister continued, "Where would you like the next meeting to be held? At headquarters?"

Larry Duckworth shook his head. "So far as I'm concerned, if I'm in the office someone will want to contact me – and it will always be of the greatest importance. The times I hear, 'I wouldn't interrupt you but . . .' "

The others nodded their agreement with Duckworth.

McAllister said, "Would you like to come down to my place in Hampshire? The air is fresh, the flowers are in bloom, and it's quiet."

"That sounds good to me. Dorset and Hants are adjacent," said Bill Manley. "But isn't it a little unfair on your wife?"

"She'll be delighted to arrange lunch for us."

"That's what we all say," said Hugh Fairley, "but we never ask our wives in advance."

"I promise you it's true in her case," said McAllister.

"How many meetings will there be altogether?" asked Lawson.

"I can't say at this stage; we may have to discuss some

subjects over a couple of meetings. But I'd say six or seven."

"Then why not let us all take it in turns and have the meetings in our homes?"

"A good idea," said Fairley.

"I think so too," said Manley, although not with quite the same conviction as the others.

"All we have to do, then, is to fix a date or dates."

Hugh Fairley said, "And I shall have to motivate my children to keep quiet. And if I succeed in that, I really shall have achieved some success in motivation!"

3 Motivating Forces

When Don McAllister's father first saw The Grange, in the village of Dogmersfield, he knew it was the ideal retreat for him and his family.

The area was rural with a typical country public house on the corner of the junction where the roads to Winchester and Sandy Lane met, and The Grange was in Sandy Lane. But McAllister senior rarely stayed at his country house, and by the time his son Donald had taken over the European Consultancy Group, Dogmersfield village had become only one-quarter rural and three-quarters built-up area.

Donald, his wife Susan, and their two children, a girl of fourteen and a boy of twelve, delighted in their occasional visits to The Grange, as a change from their London flat.

The directors travelled together in Tom Lawson's Jaguar, arriving punctually at nine-thirty am. Don acted untypically of the driving, thrusting, American businessman, and was obviously in no hurry to commence the meeting. Again, he wanted the directors to relax.

The children were away at school and Susan had prepared coffee and tea for her guests, believing that the English always preferred tea to coffee. All of them asked for black coffee.

There was the usual innocuous talk; the problems of driving to London and admiration for the décor in the lounge which overlooked the rose garden and swimming pool.

After coffee Don suggested, once more to the surprise of the directors, that after their ninety minutes' drive from town they should walk around the garden and stretch their legs. Susan joined them, and was obviously enthusiastic about every flower and every petal – almost every weed – and her enthusiasm and the peaceful surroundings began to influence the directors. She delighted in pointing out to them the delicacy of a petal, or the ballerina sway of the stems of plants, and it was ten o'clock before she disappeared to prepare for lunch, and they were ready for work.

McAllister began, "First, let me revert to our previous meeting. You may be in agreement or disagreement with some of our findings, but if we are continually having to back track we shall never move forward and finalise this exercise. Our main conclusion was that leadership and management need not, necessarily, be akin – but leadership is synonymous with motivation. Now let's hear some views on the subject."

Tom Lawson, immaculate even in slacks and yellow pullover – they had all agreed that informal dress would be right for the occasion – answered Don's request, saying, "Are we considering motivation of managers – and we all work through the management teams in the various divisions – or are we considering motivating people generally? In fact, are we considering direct or indirect motivation?"

Don said, "Let us consider the most powerful motivators – direct or otherwise. Do you think it would be a good idea if each of you explained how you can best motivate those under your control? You, Hugh, have a great problem, negotiating as you do with trade union officials whom you have to motivate to see your point of view."

"Surprisingly," Hugh said, "that isn't the main part of my job. I am more concerned with motivating our directors to get along with each other and, of course, when staff appraisals are carried out twice a year, I am directly concerned with the executives in our teams. Possibly, they may have to be motivated to take a different line of action – and none of them can accept criticism, in fact they don't like appraisals at all, unless they are sure that I am only going to praise them. But now to answer your question, what is the most powerful of motivators; undoubtedly, in my opinion, all aspects of human relations."

Before he could continue Bill Manley, his face a little flushed and his blood pressure rising, interrupted, "For God's sake, Hugh, not again! You've already driven home your holy message on radio, TV, and in the newspapers and trade magazines. You ought to join the Billy Graham circus! No offence, Hugh, but I have told you, over and over again, it doesn't work with people on the shop floor."

Hugh, expert at dealing with people of all shades of conviction and all temperaments, smiled and said quietly, "You mean you believe that it doesn't work for you, Bill, because you believe in calling a spade not only a spade, but, more often, a bloody shovel. There's a time for a tough approach, Bill, I agree – but it isn't *all* the time."

"But you must also agree," said Manley, "that I do produce the goods. That was why the Old Man wanted me in the first place, and that's why he put me on the board. In six years I have revolutionised production by my methods. Get that, Hugh? *My* methods!"

Fairley still spoke quietly. "For the first three years – yes, Bill. But during the last three you must admit there have been problems. O'Leary was a first-class works manager at the Sheffield factory, but he couldn't work with you, so he left. Since then production has not been all that good at Sheffield."

"You've got a bloody nerve bringing that up!" said

Manley. "Mick O'Leary was fighting me from the day I joined Huntley's – and you'll remember that behind my back you told him to ignore my suggestion that he did away with the coffee and tea machines."

Lawson was smiling. Duckworth looked worried. They had heard it all before, but Duckworth, particularly, did not think it right to air their grievances before McAllister.

McAllister allowed the argument to continue. It was nothing new so far as he was concerned. At meetings where the chief executive is present everyone behaves impeccably – except for those occasions when one person wants to prove his independence and show off a little. When the chief executive is not there, however, there are no holds barred.

Finally, he interrupted, "O.K., gentlemen, it's good to know that although you all work as a team you also have plenty of independent spirit. However, Hugh, your understanding of human relations doesn't seem to enable you to motivate Bill to agree with you."

"That's right!" answered Hugh. "But he is motivated, just the same, and, although he won't admit it, he does now practise human relations. Bill can't accept direct criticism – and possibly neither can I. Bill always disagrees with my views to begin with; ostensibly, to him, motivation means either the stick, or hard cash."

"Cash certainly works," said Tom Lawson, "or incentives in lieu of cash – you ask any of my sales directors or sales managers. But what Bill doesn't appreciate is that there are three types of motivation; short-term, medium-term, and long-term."

McAllister said, "I think most of us agree with that, including Bill. Let's talk about money as a motivator and give Bill a chance to relax."

Manley could see no humour at all in that remark. He said, "You try relaxing and running factories under present conditions! All you would find out is that relaxing and ulcers do go together." And with that remark Bill Manley sat back in his chair with an air of having just admonished a group of schoolchildren.

Larry Duckworth said, "I think I know something about money as a motivator." Clean-cut, a keep-fit fanatic, Duckworth looked nearer thirty-five than forty-five. "In fact, I have made a three-year study of it in our group. My study showed that for management, substantial pay increases motivated only in the short term. They motivate because a sales manager feels uplifted by such rewards, and feeling uplifted, he will work better and not mind the long hours involved, wanting to prove himself worthy of his rise. But it is only short term. He soon reverts to working on the same lines as before, maybe to only eighty-five per cent of his possible potential. And so far as the work force as a whole is concerned, whatever the reward, it doesn't motivate."

"There, you see, you're wrong again," interrupted Bill Manley. "It doesn't motivate, that's for sure, but if you don't award it, there will be de-motivation. The work force becomes disgruntled, which leads to their not working so effectively. So you'll see that pay awards do have some indirect effect on motivation."

"I agree," said Hugh, "but we can consider non-motivators later. At the moment we are thinking of cash as a means of motivating employees to greater efforts."

"How about yearly bonuses?" asked McAllister, knowing the answer, but intent on probing every area of motivation.

Again, Larry Duckworth answered, "Bonuses aren't motivators at all. Management talk blithely about executives pulling out all the stops when they are involved in a profit-sharing scheme, or some other form of bonus such as a yearly reward on turnover. This is the nonsense which, I assume, is put about by those who would obviously like the extra reward.

"Of course bonuses are appreciated; of course we look

forward to a substantial cheque at the end of the year –
but bonuses don't motivate us to think any harder, to
plan any more effectively, to work any longer hours . . .
If a manager feels he is not being amply rewarded he will
change his job – not refuse to make any extra effort
because there is no profit-sharing scheme. Let me make
one point clear: such schemes may well be ethically and
morally correct, and they may be well deserved as an
appreciation of effectiveness – and we are all in favour of
them – but they are not motivators, they are simply part
of a remuneration package. And we are concerned with
how to motivate people."

"How about profit participation making executives
more cost conscious?" asked McAllister.

"Very, very short term," answered Duckworth. "The
day the scheme is announced deep consideration is given
to costs, and managers delight in telling their directors
how clever they have been in saving here and saving
there. But this thoughtfulness lasts no longer than a week
or possibly a month. No manager worth his salt would be
encouraged to cut costs in order that he, personally,
could receive a greater bonus."

"But there could be managers with that point of view,"
said McAllister.

"Of course there could, but such people don't build
companies."

"What about commission for salesmen?" asked
McAllister.

Tom Lawson answered, "That's a different ball game.
Commission payments are definitely incentives; commission motivates, because a salesman can show, almost on a
daily basis, greater returns for harder work. But there's
no real way a manager can react to such incentives.
Management by objectives has been tried and found
wanting. There are too many imponderables to build
extra payments around these objectives – and anyway, we
never knew a sales manager who worked more effectively

because of a profit sharing scheme, although such a scheme will, certainly, make him happier in his job."

McAllister turned to Manley. "How about productivity incentives, Bill; do they work?"

Manley leaned forward in his chair, his jaw seeming to jut out even further. "Sure! Mostly with an inefficient work force – those with weak management that allows skiving, turns a blind eye to unauthorised breaks, and accepts all kinds of excuses for absenteeism. If a work force with that kind of management is given a productivity incentive they may well work some twenty per cent harder – which still leaves them probably thirty per cent below potential. With good management," he went on, "which has the respect of the work force, productivity bonuses and incentives are usually disguised perks; but for all that, a sensible offer by a manager now and again to help the worker's pay packet – preferably one which might get round some form of government wage restriction – might be effective in getting temporary extra production. It's my view that all work forces should be paid the highest possible wages, or piece rates; then, if anyone doesn't pull his weight he should be sacked. Unfortunately," Manley smiled, "this is no longer possible under present-day conditions. But that's what should happen."

"I'd like to make a point," interrupted Hugh Fairley.

"He's going to talk about human relations again," said Manley.

"Not at this moment. My turn will come! The question I wanted to ask is this: as managers, we have all grown up with perks of one kind or another – possibly subsidised travel, free meals, company cars – even clothes allowances . . . And the workers have their perks, too. But are these motivators? When you have a man or woman of the month award, is that a motivator?"

McAllister answered quickly, "Let me take the last part first; we were recently concerned with a very well-known hotel group which instigated a man or woman of the month award, hoping that it would motivate the staff. It led to rancour, jealousy, and claims of favouritism. It is believed by some types of management that we are all so high-minded that we all strive for such an honour. Salesmen may like such prestigious awards if they are based on an acceptable measure, namely orders, but this does not apply to the majority of employees. It certainly didn't please the waiters and staff at that hotel. However, management kidded themselves into believing that they were motivating their staff. They were not. Good timekeepers are always good timekeepers; the inefficient remain inefficient. We advised them to drop the scheme, which didn't please the general manager who had thought up the idea in the first place."

Duckworth said, "You say you advised them. Are you, personally, involved in every assignment?"

"No, I'm sorry, my terminology was wrong. When I said we, I really meant our consultants. I, personally, was not involved. It was one of our regional consultants who gave the advice and the solution."

Duckworth asked, "Can you enlighten us further on a small point – although we are digressing from motivation? You are head of a very large organisation, and a part of an even larger and wealthier organisation. I once read somewhere – maybe it was public relations talk – that your consultants earn as much as most managing directors. You, then, are in a similar position to our Roland, yet you are personally involved with us. Is this because after your initial investigation you believed that our leadership qualities are not good enough, but that as we are the main board directors of a powerful group, you don't believe we would accept advice from your consultants?"

The three other directors had all voiced similar opinions amongst themselves, and looked expectantly at

McAllister for the answer.

"You are fifty per cent right," he said. "I am involved for two reasons: firstly, because Dad, as an old friend of Roland's, asked me to become personally involved; and secondly, yes, I did think that although you are all highly efficient managers you may have overlooked or forgotten some of the fundamentals of leadership which you undoubtedly used in the past."

"That's a very direct criticism," said Bill, "and I, for one . . ."

"Come off it, Bill," interrupted Fairley, "let's face it, Don may be right. We have forgotten some of the motivating and non-motivating forces raised so far, and we have only just begun the exercise. It's right for the question to be raised by us, and equally right for Don to give us the reason for his personal involvement."

Susan arrived just then, to announce that lunch was ready. It was not a hot meal, to cause subsequent drowsiness, but a cold buffet which might have been created by a Cordon Bleu chef, the delicacies all to be washed down by a light Muscadet. Susan busied herself helping to replenish the plates.

Hugh asked, "And who is the leader here, Susan, you or Don?"

"Don, decisively," said Susan.

"Susan, decisively," said Don.

Light-heartedly, they went on chatting through the meal.

After lunch, when they had settled down again, McAllister said, "Let us continue with the subject of perks. Let's have your views first, Tom."

Lawson pursed his lips, thought for a few seconds, then said, "All perks are short-term motivators. If anyone wants a larger car and is given a challenge to earn one, that person will accept the challenge and work harder to win the car, but once the car has been handed over there will be no further motivation until be believes he needs a still better car. And it isn't possible to keep giving bigger and better cars. The same applies to interest-free loans, help with school fees, free maintenance, and so on. None of these perks motivate in the long run, although they do give temporary pleasure, obviously, and that is why they motivate in the short term, both before and after the gift. They can cause problems, however, when envy creeps in and other people, perhaps undeservedly, feel that they, too, should have similar perks. Which brings me to the main problem: although perks are not motivators, they can be de-motivators if not given, and this must be borne in mind. Tough management believes that everyone should give one hundred per cent of their effort, whatever their feelings towards the company or those controlling it. Unfortunately, we're not all born that way. If someone doesn't get that special car, or is refused entertaining expenses or free BUPA, that person can be de-motivated, and can go slow for a while – and while he is slacking he can de-motivate others."

"So what is the answer?" encouraged McAllister.

"The answer is either to have a generous policy and everyone knowing at what stage they will achieve a perk, or to lay down stringent rules which cannot be mis-understood. To take away a perk is, of course, a galloping de-motivator. It all depends, therefore, on what management is out to achieve, and what they think is the best way to act under given circumstances. They should always be able to adapt to situations when necessary, but should never give way, however much of a de-motivator it may be if the person is not worthy of the perk. A little licence should be given only to worthy contenders . . ."

"And are we all agreed on that?" asked McAllister.

There were nods of approval.

"Now, Hugh, it's your turn," said McAllister.

"From a personal viewpoint, better working environments have a good effect on morale – more comfortable chairs for typists, light and airy offices, good restrooms and canteen facilities and better hygiene, will all uplift morale and, in so doing, motivate workers if not to increase production, at least not to ease off, because of imagined grievances. But one should never expect any gratitude for offering something which employees expect, anyway."

Manley said, "I'll go along with that! Never expect a thank you for providing excellent working conditions, but I can assure you that good working conditions do motivate a work force to maintain a better standard of work, and a better standard of hygiene. Where there are filthy lavatories you usually find untidy and unkempt workshops, and untidy and unkempt workers – and, usually, a couldn't-care-less attitude from management."

After some further discussion McAllister said, "We seem to be covering a lot of ground on non-motivators; shouldn't we now consider the motivators?"

Hugh Fairley said, "I could begin by talking about human relations, but I think that deserves a special session on its own, and I'd like to issue a memorandum about it first, so that we have a basis for discussion subsequently."

"Fair enough!" McAllister studied Hugh carefully. He knew he had played cricket for Cambridge, and rugby for the Harlequins. He looked a product of the upper middle classes – good complexion, clear blue eyes, square chin . . . McAllister appreciated Fairley's objectivity, and clear, logical thinking. He said, "If Hugh wants to defer matters, let us consider another angle now. Can we each – with the possible exception of Hugh – give our views on what motivates us? If we know what motivates us we shall know more about what motivates other people. How about beginning, Tom?"

Lawson said, "My motivation is clear cut; marketing is

a challenge, and it's the challenge that I like and accept. Do other people like accepting challenges? I don't know. But in marketing the results are positive; if turnover falls it must, indirectly, be my fault. But because I meet and accept every challenge – the recession was a helluva challenge – I am motivated to break new records every year. Also, it means a great deal to me that Roland appreciates the work I do. Congratulations from him inspire me for weeks. I'm also motivated by the enjoyment I get out of my work, so, Don, how do we apply my motivation force right down the line?"

"You've made some good points," said McAllister, "and one in particular which is not appreciated by all executives: you enjoy your work, and it's a permanent challenge – but bear in mind that you work under near ideal conditions. You have an extremely comfortable office, you travel first-class when possible. You press buttons and things happen, which gives you a sense of power. If enjoyment of work is so important, and if the enjoyment of challenges is so vital, why don't more firms take action to try to motivate others to enjoy their work, and to accept challenges? In the USA we have had some highly successful challenges in the work forces. Productivity bonuses, as we said earlier, don't make all that difference. But team challenges – for one team to outproduce another – that always does bring good results, and yet there is so little of it in this country."

"I'd like to come in here," said Manley. "What happens in the USA isn't the same as what happens in this country."

"It usually is," said Duckworth sarcastically, "– about ten years later!"

"I'm not concerned about ten years' time," said Manley. "All I can say is that in this country to-day, enjoyment of work does apply to some, obviously, but in the main, enjoyment and challenges as motivating forces do not apply to shop floor managers, foremen, supervisors, or workers. They don't work in ideal surroundings, however much we try to make them so, so there can't be much enjoyment on that score. And there are no challenges for them to accept – except the challenge of being first out of the works when the hooter goes."

"I must comment on that," interrupted Hugh Fairley. "We have a very good work force, and you know it, Bill. In the last three years we've had problems, and there has been some loss of regard by the workers for the management. I believe that if we are to be leaders we must lead others to a better land – to better conditions, so that they can get more enjoyment from their work. Maybe that's something we have overlooked, and if we have learned nothing else to-day, I think we can begin to think about Tom's outlook on motivation to take in work force enjoyment and challenge. And to give more enjoyment, the first thing we have to consider is better communications. In the last few years our communication has been deplorable. We've sent out too many directives. I believe we could introduce more challenges for the work force as a whole, and motivate them by making their work more enjoyable."

Tom Lawson said, "That's right, we've got ourselves into a rut. At one time we had the reputation of being a great firm to work for. Are we misleading ourselves in believing that that still applies? Let me give you an example of the results when employees enjoy their work. Why is it that the staff at Marks & Spencer's always seem to be happy and contented – always willing to help customers? My wife told me recently that she was put in a good mood all day after she had called at a Marks & Spencer store and the cashier had smiled, and willingly helped her to pack her purchases – which is something very few cashiers do these days. Subsequently, she went to the food department of a nearby store to purchase some bread, which had to be sliced by the assistant.

There was a queue waiting to be served and one man asked for another type of bread, to save him having to wait. He received a very sharp reprimand, 'Can't you see we're busy?' said the assistant. 'You must take your turn.' He looked at my wife, standing next to him, and said, 'Isn't it awful for customers to be treated like that by an assistant? She can't possibly be enjoying her work.'

"Why can't stores in similar fields to Marks & Spencer motivate their staff to give better service? Managers make the same excuses as you do, Bill; staff couldn't care less, they are only interested in their pay packets, they don't agree with management policies . . . But how can they claim justification when Marks & Spencer have proved that it doesn't apply to them?

"They spend a great deal of their time and money in improving their hygiene conditions, taking real care of their staff, and building a family spirit, although they are a public company. How can other stores make excuses for their inability to match Marks & Spencer staff? Are we making similar excuses for not spending more time and money in encouraging our employees to enjoy whatever they are doing, even if it is on a production run? Can we think of any form of competition which would be a challenge to them? Shouldn't we be looking to the USA and learning from them? . . ."

The discussion continued for some time, until McAllister summed it all up; "I think we are all agreed that people are motivated to work harder and more effectively if they enjoy what they are doing. So far as communication is concerned, I think we should leave this for now as we shall need a complete meeting to cover this subject. May I say, however, that I have visited your factories and offices, and although there definitely could be a better working environment in some of the buildings, your employees still enjoy some of the best conditions in this country, in comparison with industry in general – not that we should use that as a yardstick.

Unfortunately, too many factories visited by our consultants are quite disgraceful – it isn't any wonder the lavatory walls are covered with graffiti. In such companies the leaders don't know what motivation means.

"Your turn now, Larry. What do you think motivates you to pull out all the stops – as I know you do – in your work for the Huntley Group?"

Larry Duckworth hesitated before replying, as he always did, to make certain that he was not making an incorrect statement or inadvertently breaking a confidence. "Tom has told you," he said, "what motivates him. But that is of now. What motivated him twenty years ago, when perhaps he thought he was underpaid, or his skills were not being sufficiently well recognised?"

"That," said Tom, "has never crossed my mind. I am not money-motivated – although obviously, I like earning good money. But I couldn't work any harder if I were paid double."

"You, possibly, are unusual," said Larry. "But I'm going back now to think what motivated me just after I had qualified. As my friends here know, Don, I am rather a reticent person – I have to be. I can't be forthcoming about a new idea, for example, when I don't know the finance that might be required, or how the cash flow might be affected. In spite of my great love of sport of all kinds, and my indulgence in sport as a young man, I am, perhaps, an introvert – I am rather shy. I always felt after I had qualified that I was being pushed around – even looked down on by my associates."

Tom Lawson, listening, could not help being surprised that Duckworth was letting his hair down in front of McAllister. He had always looked on Larry as a man who would think twice before saying good morning to anyone, for fear it might incriminate him. But Lawson had already learned that there was something about Don

McAllister that caused inhibitions to fade and created an urge to tell him all one's innermost thoughts and feelings.

While listening, McAllister looked deep into the eyes of the speaker, obviously digesting every word.

Duckworth continued to explain his beliefs. "This may surprise you," he said, "but to me, one of the main motivators has been status. I wanted an ACA after my name more for the status than for what it stood for. Being a professional man meant a great deal to me. I was motivated to apply for the post of accountant at our Sheffield factory because I was given such authority that it automatically gave me status. Someone said earlier that promotions were only short term motivators. I don't believe that matters very much, because if you add a lot of short terms together, they become long term."

"That's well put," said McAllister, "and I fully agree with it. No one should overlook the fact that most motivators are short-term, but nonetheless important for that."

Bill Manley was so surprised at Larry's admission that he couldn't help blurting out, "You were the one person I never thought cared a bugger about status!"

"Does any of us ever really know how the other person is thinking?" said Duckworth. "If we are to gain anything from these meetings – and I feel, now, that we shall all gain a great deal from them – we must be honest with each other. I admit that status meant and still does mean a lot to me, and if you think about it, possibly the same applies to many others in our employ. We may gain promotion, but do we get status? Very often, promotion means very little because everyone knows what the next step up the ladder is going to be. How many times do we hear that So-and-so will become an executive in two or three years when Such-and-such retires? There is very little status with these promotions – not enough to motivate one to try and improve one's knowledge and ability, no matter how long one has been with the company. But status is different altogether. Status means authority – at least, that's what it means to me! If a manager has to ask someone every time he has to spend a few pounds or make a minor decision, as happens so often, then he has no status. All his subordinates know that he has no status and, therefore, lack respect for him. Possibly a great many doctors, dentists, and lawyers work so hard to achieve their objectives because their successes do give them status in the eyes of the world, in spite of present-day conditions. I hope I've answered your question, Don. Status, to me, entails thinking harder, working harder and wanting the respect which means so much to so many of us."

The directors continued to discuss status as a motivator for some time, all of them, excepting Manley, agreeing that often, within their own company, they did not give enough authority, and that this could affect the status of a manager, whether he be shop floor supervisor or departmental manager.

Don listened, and at one point said, "We must all remember this exercise is to make us better leaders, better motivators, and to achieve this end we have to decide how to implement our conclusions. If we don't implement them, the exercise will be a waste of time. One final question, Larry: you say that status still motivates you – in which way?"

"I like to feel," Larry said, "that I have reached a position where I am completely self-motivated. But the need for status is still there. As you know, my views have been sought by government departments, and I have been honoured by my professional peers, having been invited to be chief speaker at their recent conference. I am, therefore, still motivated to give of my best because of the status I have achieved. I am not saying I can do more. What I am saying is that without that status, I might do less."

Bill Manley said, "Good for you, Larry! It's the first

time you've spoken your mind without first weighing up the consequences. But how about status symbols – a posh office, a pricey car . . . ?

Larry answered with a smile, "I wonder if you have any reason for that question, Bill – maybe you already have your eyes on a new car. You know my views. I've fought long and hard enough to keep down that kind of unnecessary expenditure."

"But it isn't unnecessary," said Bill, "if what you say is right, and status symbols give a man standing. Then they are motivators."

Larry shook his head. "You've got it wrong, Bill. In my opinion those executives who yearn for status symbols, rather than status as a measure of respect rightly earned, are usually those who haven't the ability to achieve status in the eyes of their fellow men. In my many years both as accountant and financial director I have never known an outstanding executive who was motivated by status symbols – although I suppose a lesser man could be short-term motivated by the promise of such symbols."

They continued discussing status symbols, and decided that these were not so much motivators as sometimes de-motivators if not awarded.

McAllister glanced at his watch and said, "Tea will soon be on the way, but before we have another break it would be good to hear from Bill and Hugh." He expected Manley to be forthright and controversial, and he was not disappointed.

Manley said, "Money – bloody money!" And then was silent.

"Nothing else?" asked McAllister.

"I'll elaborate if you wish. All my life I have wanted independence and the only way to achieve that is by stacking up the cash. I'll say one thing for Roland Huntley, he pays well. It's a standard management complaint that it isn't possible to accumulate capital.

Although I'm motivated by money, I want to make one thing clear: I work hard, and I devote the best part of my time to Huntley's welfare – I don't believe that managers will work harder for high rewards, but they will feel happier and enjoy their work more if they are properly rewarded."

Larry Duckworth sighed. "But what is *properly rewarded*? We all believe we are worth more –"

Don summed it up. "Money, in itself, is not a powerful motivator, except to those paid by results. But if we feel that we are underpaid for our efforts, we cannot be motivated by management drive, exhortation memos, or even a marvellous, kindly, chief executive who is a firm believer in human relations. You're right, Bill, we don't spend enough time working out a fair reward. All too often our objective is how little we need give. Incidentally, this doesn't apply to management rewards in the USA."

"I haven't finished yet," said Manley. "There is another motivator and a very powerful one these days – and that is fear. Let's not be mealy-mouthed about it; fear is unethical and immoral but it is, still, a strong motivator. The fear of redundancy has achieved far greater outputs than the thought of a possible wage increase later in the year. And the most striking example of that is with Leylands. Michael Edwardes was rightly congratulated on the effectiveness of his leadership, but he was backed by clear government statements that if there were more strikes there would be no more cash, and there could be closures. So Edwardes was able to motivate by fear. But if he had attempted to motivate that way five years earlier, he would have failed. At that time, the demand for cars was greater than the supply. Managements throughout the country were giving way to workers' demands, particularly in the car industry. They could sell cars easily, and could inflate prices to cover increased costs. But the fact remains that nobody was going to risk an all-out strike during the times when cars were in such high demand."

Don said, "Bill, are you saying that fear has motivated you?"

"It still does – although nowadays, only to a limited extent. But, let's face it," Manley was now thoroughly warming to the discussion, "we work for Huntley's, and that means Roland. He is our concern – will he sell out? If so, we could have problems. Roland has never agreed to management contracts, his creed has been to pay the highest possible salaries and perks, and he saw no reason whatsoever to guarantee this for ever. So long as we work well we know that our jobs are safe, whether we are middle managers, upper managers, or directors. We can definitely be motivated by fear when decisions have to be made. For example, recently we decided against opening a factory in the USA. Was one of the reasons the thought that if we made a mistake, if losses piled up, Roland might decide to sell the whole group, before the effects became felt here?"

"I never knew you had such a deep anxiety complex," said Fairley. "I've never worried on that score."

"But you've all felt the same at some time, although you won't admit it. I was asked what motivated me, and I've given my answer. Money, and fear – and while we're on the subject, if we're honest with ourselves we all feel concern over the future. Roland has always told us that he is going to retire when he's seventy. Who will take over then? Now, we all feel fear again – fear that it will be the 'other fellow'. So fear motivates us to become better leaders so that that particular reward will be ours."

"You're right off the mark, Bill," said Larry Duckworth. "We're all loyal to Roland, and we shall be loyal to our new chief executive who will, surely, be one of us. And if it should be you, Bill, I shall be only too pleased to accept directives from you."

"But that's not the point," said Manley. "The point is

that you don't want it to be me – and I don't want it to be you. We're still on the fear motivation. Why don't we approach Roland now, and suggest contracts? We've all helped to build the business, and we've had our fair share of the rewards – but our share doesn't compare with what the Huntley family get. In comparison we get peanuts."

Lawson and Duckworth were obviously embarrassed by Manley's outburst but they knew his attitude quite well – they had heard it all before and to some extent had, at some time or another, all voiced similar opinions, although they didn't relish an outsider being a party to their thoughts.

McAllister said, "It's a good thing to air your views at these meetings – and I do want to assure you all that anything we discuss here that is of a controversial nature is completely confidential. So if we feel it helps the cause of motivation in any way we should all talk as freely as we wish. Thank you, Bill."

"And thank you," said Manley.

"Let's leave it at that for the moment," said McAllister. "We've all learned a valuable lesson from Bill's outspoken comments. A leader should concern himself with what, for the moment, I shall term the subconscious thoughts of others. He shouldn't always expect these thoughts to be voiced, but for all that he should try to discover the fears of other people, and, if possible, take action to alleviate them. But I think we've covered enough ground to-day. I can hear the teacups rattling. Let's stop now for tea, and that can be the end of this meeting. Obviously Hugh wants some time to explain his views on human relations as a motivator. Therefore, our next meeting will be devoted to human relations."

Hugh Fairley said, "What I should like to do is to send each of you a memorandum on the subject. We can then discuss each point at our next meeting. This will save my taking up all your time with long explanations – which most of you have already heard, anyway – because I can promise you nothing new. For all that, I hope you will find my memo worth studying."

Bill Manley laughed loudly, "O.K., Hugh," he said, "you've won. And to prove it, I'll read your memo, line by line."

Don McAllister realised that Manley was not the easiest man to get along with, but at least he had the endearing quality of a readiness to apologise – something McAllister had found was not usual in most executive directors. Could Manley possibly be the no-nonsense chief executive required by Roland Huntley? Maybe yes – maybe no! There was a lot of thinking to be done before a final decision could be arrived at.

He summed up the conclusions reached at the meeting:

1 Leadership is not synonymous with management, although ideally every manager should be a leader. Unfortunately, too many managers – especially at middle and lower levels – know little of what leadership entails; steps should be taken to put this right. A leader, however, need not, necessarily, manage anything.
2 Motivation is synonymous with leadership. The success of a leader can depend almost solely on his ability to motivate others.
3 Standard pay increases and bonuses are only, at best, short-term motivators.
4 Those who can directly influence business – mostly, of course, on the marketing side – are motivated by incentives to work harder and learn more about their craft.
5 Productivity incentives do not replace effective management. This is not a decisive way to increase production, and is sometimes offered only as a sop to workers and managers alike.

6 Special individual awards do not motivate others to emulate the winners.

7 Targets are short-term motivators.

8 Targets can be strong de-motivators unless fairly set.

9 There should be standard rules covering the rewards for targets reached so that all staff know their entitlements. This could be by salary scale, length of service, or type of work involved.

10 Good working conditions are not motivators – but if conditions are not good, there can be a 'them and us' syndrome which could be a strong de-motivator.

11 It is impossible to motivate a disgruntled labour force except by fear, which applies only under certain conditions. The cause must be found.

12 Even first-class managers and executives sometimes only give eighty per cent of their potential. Therefore they, too, need continual motivation if they are to reach ninety per cent or higher.

13 When arriving at decisions, the possibility of there being non-motivators should always be considered.

14 Challenges arising out of daily tasks are excellent motivators.

15 Enjoyment of work is a motivator.

16 Achieving status is a motivator which applies in all walks of life, although it need not be affected by the position held. A craftsman held in high esteem by management because of his skills is status-conscious, and will always endeavour to maintain his status.

17 There can be no motivation if monetary rewards are not fair.

18 Fear, under certain conditions, can be a very strong motivator, and a leader should consider the possible fears of his subordinates, and attempt to ease or eradicate them.

Shortly after this, the meeting broke up, and arrangements were made for the next session to be held at Bill Manley's house.

4　Fairley's Memo: The Motivating Influence of Human Relations in Industry

As Bill Manley said, nothing will motivate for long – if at all – when an employee believes that he or she is not being paid a reward commensurate with the effort, working conditions, and the pay of others in similar employment. If a company is losing money or is making only small profits, it is of little use appealing to the loyalty of the employees to work harder for a below-scale reward.

If, as in our case, and in the majority of efficient companies in the private sector, the rewards are recognised as fair, then – and only then – can other motivating forces come into effect.

In my opinion the best short or long-term motivator is good human relations in industry. When I first became involved in personnel management I was influenced by the psychological aspects of human behaviour; the behavioural scientists and anthropologists. Then, there was the 'harnessing of the power within us' period – which meant an attempt to control the subconscious mind. I attended touch groups, to help me feel more at home with my fellow human beings; and T-groups, intended to help me lose my inhibitions . . . My objective was: by self-improvement, to influence the behaviour of others.

Nothing seemed to work for long. Some seminars did more harm than good. It was the practical experience over several years, of trying to motivate others in every sphere of business activity, that taught me that the simplest approach to human relations was best, and that nearly everyone can be motivated by adherence to five principles. Here they are:

1 *Justifiable praise*

1.1 When Larry almost burst into my office one day, beaming with pride – and I know he will forgive me for saying that financial directors don't often beam that way – I knew he had good news to communicate. Within seconds he was telling me that Roland had congratulated him on his masterly report, 'The Financial Opportunities and Risks in Overseas Development'.

Did Larry think, at that moment, that Roland was flattering him? Did he think that he was, after all, only doing the work for which he had been paid (a typical Bill Manley remark) and that, therefore, there was no need for this praise?

Not a bit of it! He was walking on air. Nothing, he implied, was going to stop him doing an even better report on 'The Financial Reconstruction of the Huntley Group'.

1.2 Bill Manley is Yorkshire, through and through, and he believes that if you praise anyone the next thing you will receive is a demand for a wage increase. Does he set himself above others? Three years ago after he had achieved almost miracles of production after reconstruction, we had a celebration dinner. Representatives of all classes of the work force were invited, and it was a foreman, representing the supervisory staff, who said "Bill Manley is the best works boss I have ever worked with – not under, mind you, but with."

Bill lived on that part of the speech for months, and every time he repeated it, ostensibly to show the relationship between management and work force in the Huntley Group, he almost blushed with pleasure – and Bill doesn't blush easily!

1.3   At board meetings we all take it in turns to refer to
some outstanding characteristics of Roland's – his insight
into the minds of others, his powers of analysis, his
objectivity, his ability to pinpoint the crux of a situation
. . . These are all repeated over and over again, but does
he object? He glows, if only momentarily, and I am sure
he is motivated to carry on with his excellent practices.

I could give similar examples applying to Tom, and to
me. The question is this: if praise does so much for us,
why are we all so miserly in dispensing it? And we are
miserly! As we become more important and our image as
top executives grows, we tend to become too ready to
accept the extra efforts of our managerial teams as
something to be taken for granted. Bill will growl, on
reading this, that no one likes a flatterer – but he doesn't
think it is flattery when the Old Man praises him!

However, we aren't considering flattery – only justifiable praise. And only a fool of a businessman flatters in
the hope of motivating others. No one likes liars, and the
flatterer is a liar.

Bill has often said that the giving of praise brings about
a request for more pay. This is not true! In all my years as
a personnel manager I have never known anyone to ask
for extra cash because of praise given for working beyond
the call of duty.

Now for some quotations. (Sorry, Larry, I know that
you object to quotations in reports; you have so often said
that if you can't make out a case, why fall back on
someone else to help you. The answer is in the humility
of man – or should be – to know that others are able to
put matters in a much truer perspective. For example:)

General Smuts once said: *Praise can bring colour to the
drabbest of lives; it can make a life worth living, and help a
man to success.*

These are the words of a great leader, and are more

readily acceptable than mine. But in more recent years, Peter Black, the well-known journalist and TV critic, wrote: *I am very fond of praise, by which I mean a compliment that the receiver knows is 'earned'. As a lubricant and a stimulant, praise is so undervalued, it is the ingredient that supplies motivation and power. It is the distilled water which tops up the flat batteries of life. But there is not enough of it about . . .*

Now you couldn't have expected me to put it as well as that!

Well, we've not learned the lesson, even though many years ago the multi-millionaire Charles Schwab, known as The Steel King of the USA, when asked to give the secret of his success answered: *Give praise when it is due – and give it lavishly.*

The other day I was talking to the restaurant manager in one of the leading London hotels. I said to him, "You always look as though you are really enjoying life – but then, so you should. You don't have to fawn on anyone; the rich, the titled, the film celebrities, are always delighted to be recognised by you."

He answered, "But it means very little to me. Because of present conditions I now do the work of three men. It is almost as if I were back in my days as a station waiter. Sometimes I am a receptionist, sometimes I help out at a station, sometimes I even help as a wine butler; but for all that I have done I have never had one word of praise from the management. They don't seem interested, so long as the work gets done."

"If they had praised you," I said, "would you have felt better?"

"Very, very much better," he replied. "I shouldn't mind any of the extra work and, possibly, the lowering of my status at all. The fact that what I do is appreciated would make it all worth while."

To praise people doesn't mean that you want anything from them – not even extra work. You praise, because it is the right thing to do. If extra activity follows – so be it!

Let me give you another example; except for Don, the rest of you know the story of our telephonist-receptionist, but it is worth repeating, because you have probably forgotten it. She had been heavily criticised for the way she answered the telephone, in spite of instructions. Then Tom Lawson telephoned one day and she gave an immaculate performance. When he arrived at the office next day he said to her, "I have never had a better reception when 'phoning head office. You were polite, you serviced the call, and you did everything you could to contact my secretary. Your voice sounded fine too."

From that day onwards, that telephonist improved tremendously – she tried to live up to the words of praise. But this applies in all walks of life. The judge is no different when he receives praise from a superior court, for a brilliant summing up. He may have a dry-as-dust personality, rarely credit anyone with good intentions – yet he will believe the praise. The famous surgeon is delighted when, after performing an operation with great skill and delicacy, he hears words of praise from his colleagues. Even the shop floor grumbler – and there are always a few of those about – will stop grumbling for a while if he is given justifiable praise. But it must be justifiable. We have all heard these remarks: 'They don't appreciate me . . .', 'They treat me like a number . . .' – people, crying out for praise.

Only strong people will praise regularly when praise is justifiable. The weak are often niggardly in their praise, for fear of building up others who might rival them in the eyes of management.

Our enemies flatter us – slap us on the back and even, sometimes, fawn upon us. But when a colleague praises us and we know it is deserved, we feel all the better for it.

2   Honest appreciation

Besides enjoying justifiable praise, we all feel the need for honest appreciation of our efforts, and the style of the appreciation can vary enormously.

A curt 'thank you' from Bill Manley can mean as much as more fulsome appreciation from others. When someone works extra long hours to complete a task, he may not need praise, but he has got to feel that his effort is appreciated and is not taken for granted.

To some, it may seem easier to get interest-free money from a moneylender than a thank you from a manager. If it is a fact that we all like to be appreciated, isn't it a mystery that we, as leaders, so rarely show our appreciation to others?

In a survey carried out by my Personnel Research division at our Gateshead factory, high on the list of causes for discontent came lack of appreciation for extra efforts made. So at that works, men and women did as much as, and no more than, basic requirements.

We eventually put forward a scheme for changing their attitudes, and undoubtedly it is now beginning to work. Incidentally, this applied particularly in the offices.

So often, management will ask someone to 'Try and get this off to-day – it's urgent!' or 'Make certain it catches the earliest post' or state that 'In view of the holidays we must have a stock of X by Friday . . .' or 'We've just got to get the stock down!'

These are requests, not demands, because a demand can so easily be frustrated – as most managers know. But all the employee would want in return for that extra effort (provided his pay is reasonable) is a 'thank you', to show appreciation. I believe that all leaders – and this applies particularly to each one of us – should set an example by giving honest appreciation wherever it is due. Appreciation motivates!

3 Criticism

A few remarks we have all heard:

'I appreciate someone criticising me' (Liar!)

'I can take it, and I can dish it out' (He means he can dish it out!)

'Am I wrong?' (He wants to hear you say he is right.)

'Tell me the truth' (He wants you to agree with him.)

And this is the way some people feel when they are criticised; a person may smile, but the smile only disguises his annoyance.

A person may say that his back is broad – but what he means is that really, it is only broad for praise but very narrow for criticism.

Then there is the person who walks out of an office apparently agreeing with the criticism. But a few moments later he will be angrily explaining to his colleagues how unfair the criticism is; and later, to his family, he will talk in even stronger terms.

Of course there must always be criticism. How else can mistakes be rectified and misdemeanours recognised? But if it is a proven fact that we are nearly all motivated by praise and de-motivated by criticism, why criticise unnecessarily?

Laurence Sterne wrote in *Tristram Shandy*: 'Of all the cants which are canted in this canting world, though the cant of hypocrites may be the worst, the cant of criticism is the most tormenting.'

Those who criticise while pretending to be helpful are often giving vent to spite. There are always those self-centred, unimaginative, thoughtless people who believe that they have the divine right to criticise and that their caustic remarks are welcome. Unfortunately, there is no cure for such people – they cannot possibly see themselves as others see them. We can only ask ourselves if we are numbered among them.

Let me make my case a little stronger; no author or playwright likes paid critics, unless they give praise. They certainly never agree with criticisms. Sometimes they write sharp letters to the press, complaining about being unfairly treated. If the critic should deign to reply, his invective is usually stronger than ever. That, possibly, is why no statue has ever been erected to the memory of a critic. Try writing to the editor of a paper criticising an editorial – and remember, editors spend their lives criticising others. Can editors accept criticisms of themselves? Not at all! They write a final reply, before declaring that the correspondence is ended; and that final reply will state very clearly that the editor is right.

I shall not touch on criticism in our private lives, because we know how annoyed we feel when friends, neighbours, or relatives criticise anything we do, or have – our gardens, our furniture, our paintings, our cars, or our holidays.

When we, or our managers, criticise unnecessarily, we do it often by memorandum. Surely it's about time such memos were banned from the Huntley Group! It's difficult enough to persuade others of the justice of our criticisms when face to face, and using the spoken word. A smile, a benevolent look can all help, but there is no smile in a letter, and if in a letter or memo, a statement *can be* misunderstood it will, surely, *be* misunderstood. And bitterness will always be the result.

4 *When criticism is essential*

The problem is deciding when criticism is essential, or when it is best to say nothing. A minor criticism is acceptable if praise has been given to cover ninety per cent of someone's activities, and the criticism only affects the remaining ten per cent. If we criticise in an acceptable manner our criticism is seen to be fair, and we have pointed out the good aspects of the person's work as well as the bad. Although we shall be disliked momentarily, it will only be short-lived. But if we criticise harshly, the effect will last for a considerable time.

If, in exceptional circumstances, we must criticise

harshly, then it must be done in the privacy of our office, never in front of a third party. Too often have I heard shop floor supervisors criticising workers in front of others or, perhaps, worse, using sarcastic remarks, which is disguised criticism. In the past this sort of remark has led to blows, even strikes. It can certainly cause a temporary reduction in output.

Let us make it a rule that there will be no public reprimand in the Huntley Group. Let us explain to our managers right down the line, so that they are aware of the problems caused by unnecessary criticism.

5   *Admitting mistakes*

The fifth principle in basic human relations can be summed up in two expressions:

I am sorry

I was wrong

– words which sometimes seem so difficult to voice. Why? Is it because to admit a mistake implies some inadequacy?

Managers, whether floor supervisors, departmental managers, or managing directors, sometimes use sentences to denigrate someone. They are said with a shrug of the shoulder, and followed by, 'O.K. then, if that's the way you, personally, feel about it, I'm sorry!' or, 'All right, if you insist that we can't produce more, against all the excellent advice I have received, then I suppose I'm wrong!'

Both remarks then become sneers, tinged with sarcasm. Admittedly, it takes a degree of strength to apologise and admit a mistake, but people with that strength fully understand the motivating force of such an apology.

The standard expression on the workshop floor – and in the office, for that matter – is: 'That bastard will never admit he's wrong!' And when that expression is used, it immediately sets up de-motivation.

We are concerned solely with motivating others, and to admit when we are wrong can be a strong motivator.

At our next meeting I expect some emphatic criticisms of my beliefs that the five basic principles of human relations are great motivators. However, the subject should be taken in conjunction with leadership by example.

May I suggest, therefore, that both these subjects are discussed at our next meeting?

Hugh Fairley

5 Motivating by Example

Alice Manley was Bill's second wife, an extremely asser-tive woman, always ready to tell Bill when he was wrong – even when he was right. Their two sons, Malcolm aged seventeen and William aged nineteen, had been brought up in their mother's image. Bill was not king in his own castle.

For days before the meeting, Bill had been pleading with Alice to ensure that the boys were away from home on that day. He did not think they would create a good impression on McAllister. But Alice would have none of that, accusing him of not being proud of his sons and adding, as she always did on these occasions, that he probably wished he was back with his childless first wife so that he would not have the expense of bringing up the children.

Alice had been the cause of his divorce twenty years earlier, and as soon as they were married she had started – and won – the battle of the sexes. Bill, a rough, no-nonsense Yorkshireman in business, was very much the henpecked husband at home. That, possibly, was one of the reasons why he was not fully convinced of the motivating forces of human relations in industry.

The Manleys lived in a rambling old house in Ealing, built at the beginning of the century, and Bill had spent a great deal of time and money bringing it up to date. They also owned an apartment in the south of Spain.

Of one thing he was sure: he could always rely on Alice

to act the loving wife when she met any of the directors of Huntley's. She wanted Bill to be admired as a family man, she knew that Roland Huntley liked family men around him, and that, possibly, Bill would be managing director one day. But still she refused to keep the boys at a distance for the day of the meeting – a perversity in her nature which, Bill felt, was either because she always wanted to do the opposite to his wishes, or else maybe it was just mother love. So Bill did the only thing possible: he lived up to his belief that money was the best motivator, and gave the boys enough cash to travel in comfort to a pop music festival that was being held in Holland. He did not want to give McAllister the impression that he could not manage his own children when he had always insisted that the cure for other people's children was more discipline.

When the meeting began, at nine am in the library of which Bill was so proud, his co-directors, who had never visited him in the six years he had been with the Group, congratulated Alice and Bill on their lovely home and regretted that they would not be meeting the boys.

Don McAllister opened the meeting saying, "An excellent memo, Hugh. It will, undoubtedly, save a great deal of our time. So many books have been written on the subject. Some are too academic, some try to turn human relations into an abstruse scientific subject. The problem, of course, is that many will claim that although it is applicable, it is difficult to put into practice. Others, possibly the majority, will not find it hard to incorporate the five principles into their way of life.

"I don't think we are going to have a very long discussion. I am glad, therefore, that we are also covering leadership by example. Now can we have your comments? Who's going to begin?"

Tom Lawson said, "I agree with Hugh, and he knows that I have always believed in the strong motivating force of his five principles. He gave the example of my contact with one of our telephonist-receptionists, but I could, if asked, give you many, many examples of the motivating force of the five principles in the sales organisation. Undoubtedly salesmen, field sales managers, and supervisors do make a greater effort when praise is given when it is due, and when appreciation is shown for their endeavours. I have seen weak men grow in stature, and strong men stride out even more purposefully, when they have been made to feel important or when someone has sought their advice."

"You've almost repeated the memo," said Manley, drily.

"You don't agree with it, Bill," said McAllister.

"Of course I agree with it! I've explained my views to Hugh, over and over again. While it may well be practical in the sales and marketing division, it is not so feasible on the shop floor. I, and many others like me, especially up north, are blunt people. We speak our mind. If someone is wrong we don't mince words, we tell 'em so – they know exactly how they stand. If they're doing a good job – that's what they're paid to do. The work force understand that attitude."

Hugh said, "You're wrong, Bill – and you know it! You're blunt – and that's not a bad characteristic, provided the bluntness is not an excuse for rudeness. There's nothing wrong with bluntness when bluntness is required, but the vital words are *when required*. So often, bluntness can be an excuse for giving force to our own convictions. But in your case, Bill, when someone has worked hard to complete a job and has failed and is then told to 'get your arse off the chair and get stuck into it' he isn't motivated to work harder, in spite of the bluntness. If, on occasion, that person has been praised for the good work he has done and is shown how to get the job done quickly, he will, nine times out of ten, respond. And Bill, you know as well as I do that in spite of your bluntness the work force like you."

"Do they?"

"You know they do, because they know you are a blunt person and when you praise them – as you do – and when you appreciate an extra effort, even if you seem to do it almost grudgingly, it is appreciated all the more because it comes from you."

McAllister thought how brilliantly Hugh was handling Manley.

"That's as may be," said Manley, but his face had flushed slightly with pleasure, "but don't tell me that you can win over the militants by making them feel big, or easing off on the criticism!"

The directors were listening intently, fascinated by the discussion.

Hugh answered, "I have been in personnel most of my working life, and I have dealt with as many militants as you, Bill – and I have won more battles than I have lost. But I do admit that if you are up against a militant who wants to show off in front of the other members of his team or committee, then no amount of human relations will help. But never run away with the idea that such leaders are immune to praise. They also need it – they like to feel important, and what happens so often at meetings is that management sets out to deflate their image in front of their comrades. That leads, inevitably, to a tough battle. But again, I agree that a few dedicated militants, with closed minds, whether they be of the Left or Right, can only be swayed by tough bargaining. But Bill, these are the minority, and I want to emphasise that the vast majority of those we deal with are receptive to the five principles of motivating people. I agree that management has to be tough on many occasions – very tough – but if this toughness is allied to the principles of human relations, it can work."

Suddenly, Bill thought of his two boys – of his constant emphasis on discipline, of his constant criticism of them, of his constant refusal to give them any form of credit for anything.

"O.K., Hugh," he said, "I'll go along with your ideas if that's the general opinion. I presume this is going to lead to some form of training scheme – but I warn you, I can't alter my personality!"

"You don't have to," said Hugh.

McAllister said, "Let's get back to basics. All we are concerned with is trying to improve the motivation of people through better leadership. If it achieves that end, then we must take action. But let us move on. Larry, it's your turn."

Duckworth answered, "There can be no disputing the validity of Hugh's arguments, only of our ability to carry out these principles. What I have learned in my profession, and in business, is that likes and dislikes are as rampant as they were when we were at school. Age and experience have not taught us how to overcome our dislikes, although we can now disguise them better than we did as school children. A dislike may have a factual basis, or it may be psychological – a different culture or religious background, manner, appearance – but it can influence our minds about a colleague. It only wants a secretary to say to her boss that Mr X is so good looking he really has sex appeal, for the boss to feel that this is an indirect indictment of his own macho personality, and is enough for him to begin to form a dislike for Mr X.

"In our computer division Arthur Blakey, the manager, cannot say a good word about John Elliot, his second in command. I believe the reason for this is that John is a better technician than Arthur, and Arthur is jealous. I shouldn't think Arthur has ever praised John – and I don't think he ever will. How do we overcome that? In private life, our lips remain tightly sealed when a neighbour, whom we don't very much like, shows us his roses and expects praise. How can we teach the five principles when so many managers find such difficulty in giving praise when it is due to someone they dislike?"

McAllister looked expectantly at Hugh.

After a moment's reflection Hugh replied, "Surely we must all realise that we can't hope for 100 per cent success with any of our motivators, and this applies even to Tom's salesmen's incentive. We may believe that we are being exceptionally generous in an award to a manager, for example, but he may have been expecting more and is, therefore, temporarily de-motivated. We know that we can't motivate hard liners in any way. For example, there is no way the five principles can motivate a militant Fleet Street print worker to ease his demands. But we are a nation with a work force of some twenty-four million people, and the vast majority are motivated by the five principles, so if we are successful with the majority – especially in our own group, and that is what we are concerned with – then I believe we can hope to achieve better results and make a lot of people happier in their work."

"I accept that," said Larry, "so long as we know that we are going to have some failures."

McAllister said, "Let's leave it at that, then. There's no need for me to be continually reminding you that we're dealing with basics. There is very little new in leadership or management techniques, but it is these basics that are forgotten. I include myself in this, and maybe you will include yourselves, too. It must be worth the effort to try to motivate others by teaching the five basic principles, but how can we implement our findings? We are only at the beginning of our discussion, yet we have already covered a fair amount of ground. We have to consider how to involve your managers in our findings so that they, in turn, will motivate their subordinates."

Lawson said, "First we have to be sure that we are carrying out the five principal concepts of leadership. We've all walked through factories without glancing at anyone. We've all been tough on occasion, just to impress others near to us – and toughness can mean needless criticism. But we have to set an example and we have to train our management staff. That comes under your training division banner, Hugh."

Hugh Fairley answered, "Maybe we should discuss training more fully later, but I should like to give Don some facts – all managers, and many members of the work force, attend various courses run by our training staff. They cover a wide area, but I believe that our leadership courses could be improved. They are too academic; we hardly touch on human relations – except to drum home the age-old views of Herzberg and Maslow. Even our case studies are adapted from those of others – and those others were adapted from their predecessors. I don't think we have developed an original case study for some time, and I'm to blame for that. I should like to suggest that we, the main board directors, run the courses on leadership for our senior directors."

"I couldn't –" began Larry.

"You don't know what you can do until you try, Larry. But in the main the courses would be run by Tom and me; we have both been involved in training over the years. And, of course, it would be wonderful if Don would also take part."

Don nodded. "I'll do that," he said, "so long as you all remember that it will add to my consultancy fee."

They all laughed – but they knew Don meant it.

McAllister continued, "It's a splendid idea, Hugh; it really is the only way to implement our findings. Memoranda won't do it."

There followed a general discussion on how the five principles could be taught, and what case studies could be used. They broke early for lunch, at twelve noon.

Alice, a dedicated organiser, had decided that they would use the lavatory from twelve to twelve-fifteen. Then at twelve-fifteen cocktails would be served, until twelve-forty-five, when lunch would be served until two o'clock.

Bill had tried to persuade her that they only required a snack, but she would have none of that! She knew she was a good cook, and she was determined to give the directors a meal they would remember.

Bill gave way. He knew he couldn't win.

The directors talked of this and that as they had their drinks, and then did their best to enjoy the heavy but very well cooked meal. While they were eating, Alice regaled them with her general knowledge of events ranging from sport to politics. She wanted to show that she could be a worthy wife of a managing director.

The meeting reconvened at two-fifteen, by which time they were all wishing that they had not eaten so much; but they looked forward expectantly to the next session, which McAllister started off by saying, "We are now going to consider motivating by example. I think, if we each take it in turn to ride our pet hobby horse and tell of the leadership example that has most motivated us, we can then put them into order of priority later. Now, someone has to start."

"How about you, Don, for a change?" said a beaming Bill Manley, feeling both benevolent and happy at the thought that his fellow directors and Don McAllister were most impressed by the sumptuous meal provided by Alice.

The fact that they were not impressed, and had long passed the phase when they would even enjoy a midday expense account meal, would never be known to Bill.

There can be so much happiness, thought McAllister, *through not knowing.*

"Very well," he said, "I'll begin: my example emanated from my Dad, who really is a great leader of men, and he has motivated me throughout my life by his enthusiasm. Every new concept, every conference he has attended, every meeting with a new client, fills him with enthusiasm. And it's catching. There's an old tag which runs: *There is nothing so contagious as enthusiasm – except the lack of it.* It's the lack of it that I want to talk about. I am not criticising anyone here, although I am criticising average British management."

Hugh knew that he was using the oldest technique in the human relations world: pretending to criticise others rather than criticise someone direct.

McAllister continued, "The British manager is, sometimes, so damned unenthusiastic, and his subordinates are often moulded by this attitude. In the States, however, a new idea is nearly always met by tremendous enthusiasm – everyone concerned becomes involved, everyone is keen to try it out.

"There is another old tag which runs: *People are paid for what they do between nine and five – they are promoted for what they do between five and nine.* Taking work home is rarely due to enthusiasm; often, it is caused by bad time management. But thinking creatively after hours is usually symptomatic of an enthusiastic outlook. If enthusiasm is lacking, who is to blame? Surely, it must be the top executives; if the managers cannot feel creative enthusiasm, they cannot possibly pass on any enthusiasm in their work force. There isn't, here, the excitement of someone shouting, "Boy! Now we're really getting somewhere!" It's more often, "They," pointing upwards, "have decided that we should . . ."

Duckworth asked, "But how do you turn unenthusiastic people into enthusiasts? I'm thinking of some of my accountants, and the workers on production lines."

McAllister answered, "You can't change people, just like that! But you can draw out from them characteristics that they already possess. Everyone waxes enthusiastic about something – sport, holidays, gardens, fishing, reading, children, left wing politics, right wing politics, music or even just beer. What we, as leaders, have to do is harness that enthusiasm in another direction. The first step is to make every worker feel that he is no longer just a cog in the wheel. Basically, it comes down to enthusiastic communication."

"Does this apply to Huntley's?"

"I don't know," replied McAllister. "You must judge. One point I must make: you can be enthusiastic, and disagree. Many a long argument I have had with Dad, but that never interfered with his enthusiasm for his cause, nor my enthusiasm for mine. I am enthusiastic about working alongside you. I am enthusiastic about these meetings. Like Tom, I enjoy everything about my work. You may say, that's fine, but what if you don't like your work? That is a case of which comes first – the chicken or the egg? If the managers are not enthusiastic there is little chance of the work force enjoying anything they do. How many times have I heard a British manager say, after reading a memo, 'Oh God! It's another bloody meeting!' – which can only mean that the previous meetings must have been awful, unenthusiastic and uninspiring. So why should they get a gleam in their eyes at the thought of yet another such offering? But let them attend a really enthusiastic meeting and they will feel inspired, and they will want to attend another. Don't try to tell me the British are different – they are not. In fairness, I must tell you that a recent survey showed that the majority of German employees also no longer enjoy their work – their enthusiasm has gone. And why? Because management enthusiasm of ten or twenty years ago has disappeared.

"Here is a golden opportunity for British management to begin to bubble with enthusiasm, to get excited about increasing productivity, or new ideas put forward by employees and, of course, by orders received. You can always tell an enthusiastic manager. He visits the order department first thing every morning.

"I have found there is usually great enthusiasm amongst employees in the smaller companies. It is in the big groups that, sometimes, managers gripe as much as the shop floor workers. I have known many chairmen of companies much more enthusiastic about being on this or that Government or Trade Association or committee or going overseas on some trade mission, than they are about their own company's activities.

"That's my example. My Dad motivated me by his enthusiasm. Now I do my best to motivate my team of consultants by my own enthusiasm. I received a letter a few weeks back from the managing director and chief executive of one of your most powerful multi-nationals. I've brought it with me." McAllister took a sheet of paper out of his pocket and read an extract: '. . . Your John Reynolds and Peter Larkin were so enthusiastically involved with *our* work – not theirs, but *ours* – that their enthusiasm was certainly contagious, and our managers willingly worked with them a long time after normal hours, to solve problems. I am also certain they all benefited by the inspiring meetings held.'

McAllister replaced the letter in his pocket and said, "That's what I *call* enthusiasm!"

Suddenly, as if rehearsed, the directors applauded. It was quite spontaneous. McAllister's example had enthralled them, and it certainly cured their after-lunch drowsiness.

McAllister smiled broadly and said, "Thank you. You picked on me, Bill, so now I'm picking on you! Let's hear your example."

"It's exemplified by our chief executive, Roland Huntley. I do want to make it quite clear that nobody holds Roland in higher esteem than I do, but that doesn't mean that he is perfect.

"I think he de-motivates by unfairness. Several times I have told him that I don't think he has been fair in his condemnation of others or his criticism of production at one or other of our factories. He ignores figures when he wants to, but uses them to bolster his arguments when he thinks it necessary. He admits that it isn't always possible to be fair, and sometimes, there is no black or white, resulting, possibly, in an unfair decision."

Hugh Fairley thought how lacking in common sense Bill was to criticise Roland Huntley at that stage. Larry Duckworth thought the remark typical of Manley, trying to show McAllister how honest and objective he was by criticising his boss.

McAllister thought how easily Manley could have made his case for fairness without involving his chairman and managing director.

Since thoughts cannot be transferred, Manley, oblivious of the impression he was creating, continued, "His unfairness has made me even more determined to be fair to my colleagues, and my work force. I pride myself on my fairness and I think this has brushed off on others. And here is my other example –" He was about to continue with other examples of Roland's unfairness when Don held up his hand and said, "You've made your point, Bill."

"That's all I wanted to do," said Manley. "We should all bend over backwards to be fair to each other and to our subordinates."

Lawson said, "When Roland appears to be unfair on occasion – and it is only a very, very rare occasion – he usually does so for a good reason. He never does anything without good reason. But where you are right, Bill, is that we are, often, unfair when others annoy us, sometimes because they are right and we don't like being reminded that we are wrong. Or we can act unfairly because we lose our temper and become too emotional, and then we make an unfair statement. We shouldn't do it, we should be grateful to Bill for emphasising the point that fairness does motivate. Bill can be difficult, but he is always fair, and I am sure that his work force are motivated to do that little bit extra for him, because of his fairness."

McAllister said, "Thank you, Tom; now it's your

turn."

Tom said, "I want to praise someone who is fair and who has total integrity. I am referring to you, Larry. As financial director you, possibly, have the most difficult job of all of us. We are all rather like Oliver Twist – we keep asking for more, and we get mad with you when you advise Roland to say no. But we know that you only ever act in the best interests of the company – even Bill will admit that you are always fair – and we can't accuse you of spending the firm's cash unnecessarily. You are always very tough on employees' expense accounts, especially for hotels and meals out, but you are even more tough on your own expenditure. Whenever you travel abroad you always find ways of saving the company's money. Your own staff, not only in your accounts office but all those down the line who know you, trust you implicitly."

"Stop it," interrupted Larry Duckworth, "you're laying it on with a trowel!"

"You're wrong, Larry; this is justifiable praise, in order to make my point. You have had an effect on me, as I am sure you have on others. I have never fiddled – at least, I don't think I have. All sales and marketing executives are apt to entertain, and spend money perhaps recklessly, and then insist that it was all in a good cause. But your attitude has meant that most of us have cut down on this wastage. So your attitude, this leadership quality of yours, has brought results. You have that very precious asset, integrity. We all talk about it, but so often we compromise, believing that there are degrees of honesty. Of course, Roland, himself, has great integrity, and that may have rubbed off on you. But for me, you have set a fine example."

Larry said, "Thank you very much, Tom, but I'm not that perfect! I pay my gardener cash at the week-end, and that isn't honest because I know he won't return it in his earnings to the Inland Revenue."

"Now you're scraping the barrel," said Lawson.

"No, I'm not. You can't hold me up as a knight in shining armour of integrity, because I'm not. I just try to do my best as financial director – that's all."

McAllister, realising that the conversation had gone far enough, said, "Larry, we all disagree with you. Roland told me that I could trust you implicitly – that you would never break a confidence, never gossip, never try, illegally, to by-pass the law. I agree that we all feel better for working for an executive we can trust, and your example, therefore, is excellent."

"He has plenty of other weaknesses," said Lawson with a laugh.

Larry laughed too. "Don't listen to him," he said, "that's criticism."

They decided that integrity would come high on the list of motivation by example.

"It's your turn, now," said McAllister, turning to Larry.

"And you need not now tell us how wonderful Tom is."

"You'd doubt my integrity if I did," said Duckworth, encouraging more laughter.

McAllister was pleased that all the executives were obviously working well together – at least, as well as could be expected. In the past, at similar meetings, he had had to face hostility; had seen jealousy in action; had watched anger override objectivity.

Duckworth composed himself and said, "I have always greatly admired Roland's courage. If he were an army officer and I a trooper, I'd have followed him anywhere because, like enthusiasm, courage is also contagious. And courage can, of course, also be allied to strength of character – the two go hand in hand. I have never known Roland Huntley avoid a difficult task. If an executive has to be dismissed, although it is not normally his function to carry out the dismissal, he will always insist on doing so. He never passes the buck. Before you joined us, Bill,

we had trouble, as you know, with the Sheffield factory.
Roland didn't send memos. Against all advice from the
works managers and his directors, he went along to that
factory. He was told there that if he spoke to the work
force the militants would shout him down, but Roland
went on to the platform – a collection of crates – and
addressed that work force. There was some heckling to
begin with, but his honesty won the day for him. That
needed courage. He instigated a new investment plan in
the depth of the depression – that needed courage. He
has fought for unpopular causes – that needs courage . . .
And I am sure that some of his courage has rubbed off on
me, as well as on others. Therefore, I say the example of
that courage, added to strength of character, are great
motivators. That's all."

McAllister said, "Well spoken, Larry. I'm sure no one
will disagree that we all have to be courageous at times to
be effective leaders, and to motivate others."

He turned to Hugh Fairley. "Now you, Hugh, are our
final speaker for to-day. What have you chosen as your
example?"

Hugh Fairley said, "I've made a long and deep study
of many aspects of leadership, but these meetings have
only one objective, and that is to make our managers and
ourselves better motivating leaders. Obviously, an effective leader must have other attributes – perceptiveness,
he may have to have technical expertise and, certainly,
the right temperament and staying power – but none of
these are motivators. Is being liked a motivator? We all
know that a manager does not have to be liked by
everyone in order to succeed; it is enough if he is
respected because of his management skill. But a leader
who wants to motivate others is more certain of succeed-
ing if he is liked by his subordinates. We pull out those
extra stops for Roland for many reasons, but mostly
because we like him.

"I should like to sum up some of the aspects of

leadership by example that we cover in our training:

If a leader takes two hours or more for lunch he cannot expect to motivate his subordinates not to slip out during business hours to shop.

If a leader arrives late at the office and leaves early, he cannot expect good time-keeping by his subordinates.

If a leader criticises his top management, he cannot expect to motivate his subordinates to respect him.

If a leader gossips, he will motivate his subordinates to gossip.

If a leader dislikes change, he cannot motivate people of ability to stay with his department, or his company.

If a leader will not delegate he will not motivate his subordinates to delegate.

If a leader wastes the time of other people he will only motivate others to waste his time.

If a leader takes no pride in his appearance he will fail to motivate his subordinates to give any thought to their own.

If a leader is ill-mannered, his subordinates will quickly become ill-mannered.

"As I now see the problem with Huntley training courses, it is that we teach, but do not inspire others to follow our teachings. We need to train our trainers.

"Obviously, we have a lot of work to do if we are to put our own house in order, and to motivate our managers to lead by example."

"And that," said Don, "just about sums up to-day's work. All we need decide now is when our next meeting is to be held, but before doing that, I think we should map out the ground to be covered in our next four or five meetings. Tom, what do you think?"

Tom answered, "Problem solving as a motivating force."

"Hugh?"

"Decision making and risk analysis. But I'm not sure

we couldn't lump all those three together."

"Larry?"

"We must include negotiation, because negotiating is largely about motivating."

"Bill?"

"Time management. Good time management is a great motivator – without such good management no one has the time to motivate anyone!"

"That's our next four meetings settled, then. Shall we have them in that order?"

They all agreed.

"And where shall we hold the next meeting?"

Tom said, "Debbie is off to visit relatives in Canada soon – so can I be next, please?"

They all agreed.

They then made their way to call on Alice, to thank her for her hospitality.

6 A Memo from McAllister

To: T Lawson
    L Duckworth
    W Manley
    H Fairley

The following are time-saving suggestions for our next meeting:

1   We combine problem solving with risk analysis.

2   Harvard Business School is, probably, the finest institution of its kind in the world, yet they made the mistake of using case studies which graduates often found inapplicable to the work in which they subsequently became involved. The Harvard team took action, and discarded many such studies which had previously been thought to be almost sacrosanct.

Unfortunately, many schools and trainers do not emulate Harvard, but continue with old practices. We must avoid this pitfall.

3   Prior to our meeting we should prepare case studies of problem solving within the Huntley Organisation.

4   As Hugh Fairley is involved with training, perhaps he will open the meeting with a brief outline of problem solving principles.

D McAllister

7 McAllister Reports

There was no desk in Roland Huntley's office. His favourite remark was, "I'm not a desk man – I'm an out and about man." Roland spent many days, each year, at his factories, both at home and overseas, but most of his time was taken up with those in power behind the buying scenes. This applied particularly to overseas governments.

His office was furnished with four comfortable armchairs, six high-backed chairs, and two small coffee tables. On a shelf running the length of one wall stood telephones, a mini computer, a ticker-tape machine, and electronic systems enabling him to establish contact quickly with any executive, anywhere. There was another telephone adjacent to his own well-upholstered armchair.

Sitting opposite Roland, sipping coffee, was Donald McAllister.

"Thank you for coming in at such short notice," said Huntley, politely. "I wanted to hear a progress report from you."

McAllister replied, "I was going to contact you, anyway. I knew you would want to hear at first hand that you were spending your money wisely."

"I don't know about that!" said Huntley. "Employing consultants is like advertising – it's difficult to check the end result."

"You won't get your money's worth with us," said

McAllister, "because your group is already so efficient; and our fees are the same for efficient companies as they are for the inefficient ones."

"Right!" said Huntley abruptly. "Enough of small talk – what's happening?"

"As you know, I have addressed your work force in Dorset and Yorkshire and I shall be in Durham next week. The first two meetings went exceptionally well – so I'm told by the regional directors and managers. Usually, these executives prefer to criticise consultants rather than praise them, but anyway, there's no union opposition to the investigation we are planning."

"Good!" said Huntley. "And how about the leadership meetings?"

"They're going better than I expected, although so far we have only touched on the subject of motivating leadership. You have a fine executive team, Roland – but then, you already know that. They're learning nothing new, but they frankly admit that they have been over-looking some fundamental leadership principles in their drive for greater productivity and sales. We all tend to forget that it is people in business that really matter."

"That's right," said Huntley. "Every chairman in his annual report thanks his work force for their loyalty and splendid efforts, but it's often tongue-in-cheek stuff. We, here, strive not to be like that."

McAllister said, "Huntley's definitely are not like that, but your directors all agree that there can still be substantial improvements in the field of human relations, for example. Our objective, as you know, is to motivate others to give better results."

They talked for a while about the ground covered at the meetings, and Huntley went on, "What is your next meeting to be about?"

"Problem solving and risk analysis."

"Fine! I have my own views on problem solving. I shouldn't think they're the same as yours, so I won't voice them."

"But the end result is the same," said McAllister. "You can rely on your vast experience, and your computer-like mind can quickly make assessments which others would take much longer to form. But we are concerned with your managers, and we must find them a formula to help them solve the problems they meet daily."

Huntley shrugged his shoulders. "Probably you're right. And your meeting after that will, surely, be on decision making."

"Yes."

"I should like to be present."

"Oh!"

"Not so much of the 'oh'! I know you told me at our first meeting that I should be an inhibiting factor, but I believe I can add to the value of that meeting. I have had rather a lot of experience in decision making – some of which has been extremely difficult. The majority of my decisions have been right, but some have been wrong."

McAllister sighed. "Yes," he said, "but don't you think it would be better –"

"No," interrupted Huntley. "I pay the piper – I call the tune." He laughed. "Sorry, Don, I don't really mean that, but I honestly do believe that under your guidance – and I do assure you that the meeting will still be under your guidance – I shall be able to add a little extra, to the benefit of both you and my colleagues."

"Put that way, how can I argue?"

"That's settled, then. Let me know the date well in advance. Now, changing the subject, have you been able to form any opinion, yet, of the respective merits of my directors?"

"It's really too early for that, Roland. Briefly, my conclusions so far are that Bill Manley has that toughness you admire in a leader; Hugh Fairley has the overall capacity for getting the best out of everyone; Tom is a true Huntley loyalist and is a man of great drive and enthusiasm. If you want a rock as a leader – someone who might not take the group to any great heights quickly, but neither would he immediately make changes which might prove detrimental to the group – then you'll pick Larry Duckworth. But these are snap conclusions – it's far too early, yet, to give you any worthwhile appraisal.

"But you can be sure of one thing, Roland: there will never be another Roland Huntley, so don't look for one. On that basis, any one of your directors would do a very good job as chief executive."

8   Leadership and Problem Solving

Tom and Debbie Lawson and their three children could have graced any TV commercial depicting the ideal family group. Debbie, brought up in a vicarage by parents who believed that religious faith allied to discipline would always prevail against the wickedness of the modern way of life, became a top model at the age of eighteen. A slim red-head with greenish-grey eyes, she attracted all men, but remained faithful to one. The children were Robert, a first year medical student, followed by Tina, aged sixteen, an embryo nurse; then came George, twelve, whose objective was to be the first astronaut to land on Mars. Although, like all families, they had their differences, with them they were few and far between.

Debbie had taken up jogging, while Tom still played a very good game of squash. On the rare occasions when the family happiness was slightly marred, it was due to Tom having an attack of the blues. He had always been someone who was either on top of the world or down in the dumps, finding it difficult to live with disappointments relating either to family or business set-backs. He hid his feelings very well from his business associates, but not from Roland Huntley. At the moment he was slightly on the downward slope, due to the fact that he felt he was not doing enough to impress Donald McAllister. He could not begin to contemplate working under anyone other than Roland Huntley, but knew that if the crunch came he had not enough capital behind him to consider risking any change.

He had a luxurious home to maintain, the family always had expensive holidays, the children were begrudged nothing, and he enjoyed buying Debbie expensive jewellery. If Roland kept his word and retired at seventy, Tom would be about forty-nine – and that was no age to risk making a change, unless it was forced on him. He had seen too many high-fliers make such changes, and then not produce the brilliance required by new, demanding bosses. The compensation paid for loss of office under those circumstances did not nearly make up for the extreme difficulty of obtaining another highly-paid executive post. He knew, therefore, that he had to win, but that he was up against strong competition. Manley was a born fighter – and Huntley liked fighters. And Bill had increased production substantially, in factories both at home and abroad, in the short time he had been with the company. He was also very cost-conscious – and Tom Lawson knew *he* was not in that mould. Huntley had always believed that the ruination of many companies was too much spending by departmental chiefs – and he, Tom Lawson, was known as a very free spender.

Hugh Fairley had the ear of all the directors in every division of the group. He personally had engaged or promoted many of them. If Huntley were to sound out the views of the regional boards, Fairley would get the vote.

Larry Duckworth also had many advantages – a keen analytical mind, strength of character, business integrity, and a strong grip on the financial affairs not only of the holding company, but also all the regional groups. And Roland was always on the side of the financial wizards.

When Manley had accused Huntley of being unfair, he and the others had all vetoed the very thought, but they had all been playing games. Huntley often was unfair –

often completely ruthless – and Manley was the only one with guts enough to criticise his boss in front of McAllister. Would that impress McAllister? Or would it antagonise him? Tom thought it might impress him. Huntley did not regard loyalty as a reason for promotion; his only concern was dynamic efficiency. He – Lawson – knew that on the count of dynamic efficiency he would get full marks; but he also knew that promotion could depend on McAllister's views.

Lawson's home was a home for beautiful people: a mock Georgian house in five acres of grounds, manicured lawns, fruit and vegetable gardens and, inevitably, the pool surrounded by a brilliant display of flowers. The tennis court and swimming pool were only a few minutes' walk from the small goldfish pond.

Tom Lawson, mortgaged up to the hilt, was always short of money. His colleagues had been led to believe that Debbie had come from a wealthy family, and that was why there was no need to watch the pennies – let alone the pounds. Tom had even misled himself into almost believing this story.

But in one respect he was right – and it was a great point in his favour: Roland Huntley believed that a good top executive needed a stable home life. Manley's wife was too assertive and would get involved in business affairs if her husband were in charge; Hugh Fairley had been divorced from his first wife and was now married again, but there were rumours that he was not really happy the second time around; Larry Duckworth apparently had a very happy home life, but was having an affair with an ex-beauty queen, and he wondered what Huntley thought about that. Lawson, contemplating the position, finally decided that he had as good a chance as anyone.

Looking as lovely as ever with Tom by her side, Debbie greeted the visitors, and immediately won over McAllister with her femininity and charm. The others had already met her on several occasions, and all thought Tom a very lucky man to have such a wife.

It was eight-thirty am and even as early as that it was evident that a warm June day was in store, so Debbie had arranged for the meeting to be held in the garden, adjacent to the pond. There were tables, chairs, and even a cooler cabinet containing soft drinks and ice cubes. Before leaving the pondside she said, "Tom thought you would like a snack lunch out here." They all agreed that it was a good idea, and McAllister appreciated the way she deferred to her husband.

When they were settled in their chairs McAllister said, "To-day's subject is problem solving and risk analysis. Hugh is again going to open the meeting, so – over to you, Hugh."

Fairley said, "As we are each going to give a case study all I need to do is define the standard techniques, as taught at our problem solving courses.

"First, is a standard solution available? By this I mean, has a similar problem been solved before? If so, there is no need to waste any time searching for a new solution. Obvious as this is, it is very often overlooked.

"Secondly, is there a time factor? If it is important that solutions to a problem be found within twenty-four hours, then an investigation in depth is rarely possible and, therefore, risks may have to be taken. This, if there are alternatives, calls for risk analysis, to ensure a correct decision. If, for example, there is an ideal solution but with great risks entailed, this might be discarded for a solution which may not be perfect, but is much safer to adopt.

"Thirdly, group problem solving should be adopted for tackling highly technical or innovative problems. At the Huntley training centre during problem solving sessions we cover most of the known formulae for problem solving. I shall outline them although it may seem time-wasting, but we have to keep to our mandate of reviewing fundamentals.

"At each session we form groups of about six, appointing a leader for each group. This selection is all important, to ensure that the leader is strong enough to take control but does not exceed his authority; that he encourages others to talk but is not too garrulous himself; and that he seeks to involve all members of the team in the discussion.

"In no particular order, here are the various problem-solving group discussion techniques:

"First, of course, is the standard method of each group considering all the facts of the case study provided, analysing them, and arriving at a solution. Incidentally, all case studies are based on actual problems which have occurred and for which correct solutions were found. The reversal formula is a technique which can prove valuable when deadlock occurs. It involves simply reversing solutions already considered and found wanting. For example, we hit problems with our new hand fire extinguishers. Our biggest orders were from government and local authorities. All went well until a Japanese manufacturer entered the market and slashed prices. We lost about seventy-five per cent of the tenders we submitted. We had a group executive meeting and, after lengthy discussions, we decided we would have to fight back to try to knock them out of the market. The losses over three years – the time we considered reasonable for victory – were considerable. But we knew that the profit-conscious Japs would not go on losing for ever. Also, although their extinguishers met all specifications, we felt there would be a deterioration problem.

"Then Roland joined the meeting and suggested the reversal technique. We reversed everything – size of order required to keep down production costs, increased prices by twenty-five per cent instead of reducing them, stopped tendering for government or local authority business and went for the smaller businesses and shops. We reversed again and sold not through distributors but direct . . .

"Finally, that was the decision accepted. The Japs sell on quantity. We marketed by *professional selling* allied to quality."

Bill Manley said, "Do we need to consider all these examples?"

Don McAllister quickly interrupted him. "Yes, we should all not only refresh our memories, but know how the Huntley training centre is at present tackling problem solving. Carry on, Hugh."

"I'll try to cut them short, Bill," said Fairley. Then continued, "We use the fantasy, or dream system – dreaming up the impossible. This, we have found most effective when tackling service, technical, or innovative policies. Each syndicate member lets his mind wander into what we term outer space, beyond the fringes of normality. From such fantasy thinking came a device linked with a water sprinkling system, which enables a motor to keep running and a fan to keep extracting smoke that would otherwise suffocate those trying to escape a fire.

"The sessions are often hilarious, but they do achieve their objective of stretching the mind so that its electric impulses move into new areas.

"A more normal method is to break a problem down into individual parts and give each syndicate a part to solve; then bring the whole together at one session. Recently, Syndicate A were considering whether stock was too high or too low; Syndicate B, whether suppliers should be made to cut prices or lose our business – or whether we should buy overseas: Syndicate C whether we should find storage space if necessary, or lease local premises . . .

"There were five syndicates in all – the whole objective, to cut costs."

Smiling at Manley, Hugh continued, "Just three more, Bill. The first is based on the old *pass-it-on* method, everyone adding to the thoughts of others. Small syndicates are formed and presented with a problem. Each member of the syndicate writes down his ideas for solving that problem; the papers are then passed to the right, and the recipients try to improve on their colleagues' ideas for problem solving. Eventually, there are a number of different solutions, which are each discussed until a final solution is reached. It is most effective."

Manley asked, "Are you telling me that any manager within our company carries out that exercise to solve a problem?"

"These exercises," said Fairley, "are designed to get the mind reacting automatically to problem situations. A manager might not write down anything on paper, but he will ask others to try to improve on his ideas. But in fact, enthusiastic managers have been known to go through the full process sometimes.

"The Japanese are masters of this art. When they consider problems most of the managerial staff, and sometimes all the work staff also, may be involved. It is the same basis as *passing it on*, each trying to improve on someone else's ideas."

Fairley paused for a moment, then continued, "Well, Don, here is the last exercise: it incorporates *risk analysis*. A lined sheet of paper is handed to each trainer; on it are drawn five columns. The first is headed *obvious cause*, the second, *probable cause*, the third, *improbable cause*, the fourth, *risk analysis* and the fifth, *the solution*. A problem is then set – and it should be one of which all the delegates are aware, for example, 'dissatisfaction with building work carried out in the home'.

"In the first column is written the obvious cause of the problem: 'the employment of an incompetent builder'.

"In the second column is the probable cause: 'acceptance of the lowest tender, therefore, low cost labour
employed: extra charges incurred through not reading
terms of contract carefully; poor materials used; builder
not asked to supply sample finishes; work not checked in
progress; too much paid in advance . . .'

"Under *improbable causes* could come: 'the builder had
too much interference from house owner's wife who kept
changing instructions; the builder was about to go
bankrupt . . .'

"In the risk analysis column, which, of course, is
equally applicable to decision making, might be written:
'cost of legal action too high to be acceptable; bellig-
erence would result in physical action – even arrest;
having work done by another builder and sending the
first builder the bill would only result in extra cost;
failure to pay the balance of the account could lead to
being sued, and if the case were lost, blacklisted by credit
rating agencies; writing to a local paper could result in a
libel action.'

"All the evidence is now available. Naturally, I have
made it very brief, but the delegates carry out exhaustive
analysis under each heading. The solution sometimes
given is: avoid emotional anger, wait to be sued by the
builder for the balance, and complete the work yourself;
the builder might not sue. The solution given time and
time again is to call on the builder. Never write, but call,
if necessary, over and over again, to discuss the situation,
accepting that possibly there had been rights and wrongs
on both sides – always striving to get the builder to re-do
the work himself. That is really the only way the problem
can be solved without risks, and without additional costs.
This is persuasive problem solving.

"Most people, it is usually decided, become angry or
emotionally swayed by the advice of wife, or friend, and
the builder then digs in his heels. This analytical exercise
is probably the best of all problem solving procedures.

Now for my final exercise –"

"Another final?" asked Manley.

"The last, I promise you. It is *problem solving by direct change*. This applies mostly to products. Again we ask trainees to write down their list of

(a) what changes they would like to see in the product
(b) what changes others would like to see in the product; for example, the salesman, buyer, sales promotion division . . .
(c) what they would take away from the product and what they would put in its place

We also ask:

(d) if the product were removed from the range, would a replacement be needed? If so, what kind of replacement would they like to see?
(e) if most of the product were discarded, what aspects of the product would they use as a basis for developing a new product?
(f) why do we continue with the present shape, colour, material . . . ?

"These are the main group problem solving techniques, but there are many, many more – some so difficult to understand that they need problem solving techniques themselves, to discover what the many initials used mean, let alone what the techniques entail. We eschew all unproven academic problem solving ideas. What we, the main board, have to decide is what we can do by training and example to inspire our managers to use one or another of our successful problem solving techniques.

"Our managers have to solve so many minor problems which we never hear about unless they prove insoluble, escalate, and cause headaches at head office. The shop floor difference of opinion is a typical example. If it is not solved by the manager, it can escalate. There can be a minor breakdown in the running of the plant and, possibly, a strike, if the problem is not quickly eliminated.

"You see, Don, the problems we, as a main board, have to solve are mostly concerned with major events, and we have vast experience to draw on."

"Hey now, wait a minute –" interrupted McAllister, "major problems are only minor ones on a larger scale. The same principles apply, and remember, not many firms go bust because managers don't solve minor problems. This exercise is to refresh *our* memories as much as to impart knowledge to others."

Lawson was surprised at McAllister's interruption. Then he realised that Don did not want the directors to forget Huntley's request for better leadership from the top.

Hugh's face showed his concern at the interruption, so McAllister said, "I'm sorry. We all learned earlier that we shouldn't criticise in public. I apologise, Hugh."

Fairley shook his head. "Not at all. We all do criticise in public, over and over again, in minor matters. You were not criticising, Don, only putting things in their true perspective – and that, after all, is what your assignment is all about. You are right, but may I put it differently? Our managers – a few of them below average, some average, but the majority above average – don't usually have the experience to fall back on that we have. Therefore, as I said earlier, they sometimes can't resolve problems by trying to draw on their own experiences of what they have done previously. But I do agree that irrespective of the size of the problem, the principles involved in solving it are the same."

After they had discussed each of the exercises, the cooler cabinet was opened and thirsts quenched. The sun was now high in the sky, and it was becoming uncomfortably hot, so they moved their chairs to the shade of the nearby trees.

McAllister, gulping a can of coca-cola, said, "Roland asked me to look in on him last week. He wanted to know what progress we were making."

"And, no doubt," said Manley, "what you thought of his gang of four?"

"That's right," answered McAllister honestly, although he had not been expecting such a direct question.

Larry Duckworth said, "Surely that places you in an invidious position."

"Why?"

"We're all co-operating on an exercise for the benefit of the company and apparently, now, we also have to consider how we ought to be behaving in order to impress you."

"Come off it, Larry," said Lawson. "We all know our Roland, and we all know that he couldn't resist seeking Don's opinion. He's always trying to find out our opinion of each other – it's the way his mind works, always seeking facts on which to base his decisions."

"That's all very well," answered Larry, "but are *you*, Don, going to evaluate us and give an opinion of our suitability to take over the job of chief executive?"

McAllister replied, "You are four men very wise in the affairs of the business world. You all know that when consultants are called in, they are nearly always asked to evaluate executive staff, and even the chief executive himself. Many a time we have had to suggest that a company is having problems because of the ineffectiveness of the managing director. Of course, we wrap it up, but that's what it amounts to in the end, and the result is that the managing director will either throw us out and disregard our general advice, or will consider elevating himself to president. We win half and lose half. Knowing Roland, he will consider every tiny aspect; he will go through your backgrounds with a toothcomb. He may, or may not, listen to any advice I give, but my views could never be derogatory, because you are all too good for that. So let's just leave the matter there."

"Just another problem to be solved by each one of us," said Hugh. "How are we to influence the mind of the Old Man for our future benefit?"

"One for all and all for one," said Tom Lawson. "Let us be the only company with four top executives."

"What a good idea," said Manley, "provided I'm chairman!"

McAllister interrupted. "Back to business! We, at McAllister's, are professional problem solvers – that is what consultancy is mainly concerned with. No problems – no consultants! And Hugh, in the past we have used many similar exercises to those you have outlined. The mistake in industry is that they don't use these exercises, and that is why, sometimes, they have to call us in. But for your information, this is the order in which we consider each problem:

1 Clearly identify the problem. Often, we are given a series of minor problems to solve, none of which is clearly identified with the real problem. For example, in one company there was cause for concern because of the high turnover in staff – especially sales staff. We were told that the problem was due to the autocratic style of the regional managers. Someone else told us that it was due to the salary scales being much too low. Another opinion was that the company's car policy was to blame.

"We eventually identified the real problem, which was a shocking inability on the part of the managers to interview and select staff. Applicants were often not given exact job specifications and, therefore, quickly became disillusioned when they found that they had to undertake what were thought to be possibly menial tasks. Promises were made, but were not kept. But the managers, when questioned, believed that they all had a special flair for interviewing. They certainly had not. By

identifying the real reason we were able to solve this problem by holding interviewing and selection seminars.
2 Obtain *all* the relevant information. This, I am sure, you feel insults your intelligence, but the fact is that very rarely are all the data accumulated. Snap decisions are made, and, even after lengthy discussion, decisions are made on generalisations.

"Only facts matter – facts which we can interpret when we have the overall picture of the problem.
3 When we have interpreted the facts – sometimes we call it rediscovering the facts – we discard those which are not applicable. We also ensure that there is no personal involvement with the facts presented, which usually means that the facts have been coloured by personal views.
4 Seek problem solving ideas by group discussion. The group discussions are, of course, based on those already depicted by Hugh.
5 We consider all the different solutions reached, and then evaluate them against these criteria; will solving the problem in this or that way create new problems later? If there are alternative solutions, we usually find that we choose the one which has fewer risks attached. We search also for the true costs of a solution. Costs are often hidden, or disguised because of emotional involvement or lack of thought.

"That is a very brief outline of our procedure, but I shall enlarge upon it later. Any comments?"

Lawson said, "We adopt the same procedures, but what we have to impress upon our managers is that, however small the problem, they should still keep to the set problem-solving principles."

"Right," said McAllister. "Now we can get on to our case studies. Would you like to start, Tom?"

Tom Lawson looked at his watch and said, "Debbie will be along soon with our snack lunch, but I think there may be just enough time to put my case study forward. It is based on the marketing of our fire-fighting appliances in Saudi Arabia. Bill and I were both closely involved in the negotiations with Leslie Simpson, managing director of Huntley's Exports. Hugh and Larry only came in at the final meeting, so that some of the aspects will be new to them.

"Long before the recession which no one thought would happen, we, at Huntley's, decided that it was inevitable and that we could not depend on home trade to see us through. We decided, therefore, to intensify our export drive, and chose the Middle East as our main target area – especially Saudi Arabia, already a good outlet for our products.

"After some investigation and several visits, we offered the concession to an Iraqi expatriate who had lived in Saudi for some fifteen years, and he became our agent on a commission basis. His name was Hassan.

"Within a few years our turnover had risen to several million pounds a year and then, during the height of the recession, came news from Hassan. He had obtained the sole rights for importing fire-fighting equipment in the short term, provided that in the long term he could set up a joint manufacturing company with the supplying company – us. We were to provide the expertise, the key staff, and fifty per cent of the share capital. Hassan was to market the extinguishers and, as he pointed out, with the sole rights the turnover could be enormous. The snag: we had to invest over a million pounds, and to guarantee further sums as required. That, we didn't like! But if we didn't put up the money, another manufacturer would do so and we should, eventually, lose a high proportion of our Saudi business. However we made the investment we could find ourselves in the position of a bank, which has continually to lend money to keep a business afloat. The bank would have collateral, but our collateral in Saudi Arabia would not be worth a great deal.

"The first question we asked: what is the real cause of the problem? Is it the Saudi government, demanding local manufacture? Is it Hassan's desire to gather in a lot of cash quickly? Or is it brought about by the success of a US competitor, which could cause problems ahead for Hassan and for us, unless he engages in local manufacture?

"What do you think about these factors, Don?"

McAllister answered, "I don't think government pressure would be so strong that Hassan couldn't keep it at bay for some considerable time, but he could see a way of building the business at your expense. Would he put up the other 50 per cent, or would his contribution be taken out of profits? These are questions that I should have wanted answered."

"Right! And they were our questions, too. Now for the information," went on Lawson, "which I shall keep brief. The market was still enormous. Hassan had a very good reputation, but we soon learned from other sources that such reputations in the Middle East are apt to change very quickly. He had always acted with great propriety in the past, but that was as an agent. Now, his hands would be on the till. We checked and rechecked with many independent sources, and continually we came back to the question: with money dripping all over the sands of Saudi from millionaire princes, why did Hassan want our million which, so far as the Saudis were concerned, was chicken feed? Surely any investment-conscious Saudi would be only too pleased to put up the money, if Hassan didn't have the cash himself – and we discovered that Hassan did not have the cash. Why, then, did Hassan not obtain it locally? Why did they want to share with us? We kept stalling, playing for time. We checked with other British manufacturers who had attempted local manufacture, and learned from them many snags. Then one day we learned from a friendly source that Hassan was being visited regularly by one of our French competitors. There could be only one reason for this; he was playing each of us against the other.

"The problem: should we tell Hassan what we had discovered, or should we break off negotiations? Bill Manley was greatly concerned that we should do everything to try to find some way of keeping our exports to Saudi going, at least for two or three years until we had built up our exports in other areas. Our Yorkshire factory was so dependent on Saudi business; without it, there would have to be redundancies.

"We had a brainstorming session from which the following points emerged:

enlarge the export staff and fight harder to become independent of Saudi

check again with non-competitive companies who might have been placed in a similar position

check directly with the French company to see if, as a last resort, we could co-operate with them and both share the sole manufacturing rights

keep negotiating with Hassan, as if nothing untoward had happened.

"Contracts we had already received covered us for nearly a year ahead so we only had to keep going for another year or so, negotiating all the time.

"The export division was given the go-ahead to invest more money in exporting to new areas.

"We checked with a company selling pharmaceutical products and were then, amazingly, told something we should have found out earlier, but had been unable to do so: the sole licence that Hassan would have received would have been for one year only, and if not set up within that year it would have lapsed. Also, his sole licence did not prohibit other Saudis from obtaining similar licences if the contract was so large that no one manufacturer could fulfil it. It would not have been difficult to prove to the Saudi authorities that, in fact, no one manufacturer could supply all their requirements.

"The French company's president, whom Roland knew quite well, told him that they were certainly negotiating but had not yet arrived at a definite decision. That surprised us. Why had they not jumped at the idea of knocking us out of the market? The reason could only be that they considered the venture with Hassan too risky.

"The venture would not have been so risky if Hassan had offered to put up 75 per cent of the money, which would have been the correct thing for him to have done, as he would be virtually in control, anyway. So we carried out another risk analysis, and these were some of the facts which came to light:

"We had to provide key personnel. What would happen to one of our employees in the event of some problem arising – a dispute with the Government, for example, who could then make demands which couldn't be met? Would the Saudis then refuse to give an exit visa to members of our staff until we had settled the bill? Conversely, if Hassan wanted to take over, could he persuade the Saudi authorities to refuse visas for our staff to travel there – especially our accountants, who, under the terms of the agreement, would be empowered to examine the books of the company at regular intervals? If, therefore, Hassan wanted to break the agreement at any time, he would have many options open to him, and we should have no recourse to damages.

"The main risk, however, was that once involved, how could we stop providing additional capital on demand? What if Hassan demanded nine months' credit or longer for goods we supplied from this country?

"Having considered the risk analysis, we then considered the benefit analysis:

"If we agreed to go ahead it would take at least twelve months to set up a pilot factory for assembling units, which would be the first step. During this time profits from the equipment we were exporting would give us a good cushion against future losses. If we continued on this basis of assembling for only three years we should certainly cover our complete investment – provided, of course, the Saudis played along with us.

"But they didn't want assembly plants. They wanted complete manufacturing processes. We could determine the exact amounts we were prepared to invest and cut our losses in the event of severe problems looming ahead. The benefits to us could, therefore, be highly profitable exports, for a limited period.

"You'll see, Don, that we kept to the rules fairly well. We tried to discover the real cause of the problem. We spent a long time accumulating all the relevant facts. We carried out risk analysis and benefit analysis, although in both cases I have only given brief outlines of what emerged from our meetings. We weighed the balance and decided that if Hassan could negotiate behind our backs at this stage, the risks outweighed the benefits. We decided to terminate the negotiation.

"Our export director, after some difficulties, got a visa backed by another importer. To obtain visas for Saudi, as you know, a national has to back the application. We contacted those who might like to co-operate with us if we broke with Hassan. We knew that anything that happens in Saudi at 11 am is known by everyone at noon. Hassan would learn of our negotiations and would realise that we knew of his negotiations with the French. This comes under the heading of *preventive problem solving*.

"Neither Hugh nor Don have elaborated on this, but I know that at our courses it is taught that whenever possible, preventive action should be taken to stop a problem escalating. Our mistake was probably not taking preventive action earlier. We should have foreseen the way Hassan's mind would be working. As the French had concluded no deal, we felt we were taking little risk if we now told Hassan that we were not prepared to put up

any money for a joint venture. We said we would be only
too pleased to supply the know-how and the manufacturing skills needed. We would supply the parts as required
and all that we should need in return would be a
management fee, plus a royalty on turnover. And, we
said, he – Hassan – could take all the profits from the
Saudi company.

"The decision was taken after we had discussed the
matter with the personnel involved who would have to
live in Saudi for between one and three years. They were
all willing to go out there, and were quite prepared to
take any risks necessary. They felt there would be no
risks if the Saudis put up the money.

"We arrived at the right solution. Hassan decided to
accept our terms with, of course, some slight modifica-
tions.

"Although I have only outlined the Saudi story briefly,
I believe it to be an object lesson in problem solving.

"When the offer was first made to us and we felt that
we should get sole manufacturing rights, there was
elation all round. It would have been easy to have arrived
at a snap decision. Even Bill, at that time, was urging us
to agree to Hassan's terms because it would solve a
manufacturing problem for him. But in fairness to Bill,
he did change his mind subsequently – especially when
we realised that the real cause was not the demand of the
Saudi government, but Hassan's eagerness to get rich
quick without personal risks.

"By going through all the procedures we eventually
arrived at the right decision – and it's one we have never
regretted. We may not, now, make so much profit from
the Saudi venture, but our profit is high enough when
allied to the security."

Lawson's conclusion was perfectly timed. At that
moment Debbie arrived with two girls whom she had
conscripted from the local School of Cookery, to help
with the luncheon. Each carried a tray which she placed

on the folding table which stood against one of the trees, and went off to collect more trays. They brought small melons resting on beds of ice, platters of cold ham and chicken, a tray overflowing with dainty smoked salmon sandwiches and, of course, a colourful array of salads. Once again, the cooler unit was opened, this time to extract lagers. Everyone thoroughly enjoyed the luncheon, and considered it just right for the occasion.

When they were ready to begin the meeting Tom said, "It's getting very hot, it must be in the eighties. Would you like to go indoors to continue?" They all concurred, and were finally ensconced in Lawson's study or, as he called it, his workshop. Here, there was a notable change of temperature due to the room air conditioning unit he had recently had installed. The Lawsons, thought McAllister, seemed to have everything! As soon as they were all once more comfortably seated McAllister said, "Now it's either you, Bill, or Larry. Who wants to go first?"

Bill Manley volunteered to give the next case study. "You'll have to be careful, Hugh," he began, "if you want to use this example as a training exercise. You can, of course, disguise the event, which highlights the need to look, sometimes, for the improbable cause of a problem when there no longer seems to be an obvious or probable one.

"It happened soon after I joined the company. For the first time in the history of Huntley's a strike was threatened in our traditionally moderate Dorset plant. I was then a newly appointed works director and was, of course, extremely worried."

McAllister carefully studied the production director who had so quickly achieved success and promotion to the main board. He had the face of a booth fighter, the stomach of a regular beer drinker, the mind of an outstanding engineer and the directness of a judge.

Manley was talking slowly. "It all began when we were asked by the works committee – a most moderate bunch of men – for an urgent meeting. We had already agreed the pay award for the following year, which was above the government-indicated norm, and certainly above that offered by other manufacturers in the area. We held a reputation for high pay allied to high productivity. The meeting began in the usual friendly way, then Harold Webb, chairman of the works committee, said that the boys didn't think the pay award was high enough. They wanted us to renegotiate, with a minimum extra of five per cent.

"I explained with great patience the details of the more than reasonable offer we had already made, but got nowhere. Negotiations went on for several days, then we were told that unless we were prepared to increase the offer there would be a walk-out. Webb said the boys were adamant, and the works committee could only carry out the wishes of its members."

Manley paused, blew his nose hard, then went on, "You know me! I believe in the tough approach." With a wry look at Hugh Fairley he added, "Of course, from now on I shall have to try a little harder on the human relations aspect!

"Bob Denton, the works manager, strongly advised me against confrontation at that stage, so I reverted to the standard problem-solving procedures. Denton, the financial director Alan Todd, and I, formed a committee to decide what was the real cause. You may remember that at that time the managing director of the Dorset company was very ill in hospital. Later, I succeeded him, but at that time we had to manage without his advice. First we looked at all the obvious and probable causes. The obvious was the one put forward by the works committee – that they believed they deserved more money – but was that the true cause? Were they, perhaps, discontented because of lack of communication – the 'them and us' syndrome, which might have been aggravated by my arrival? Were they discontented because the charge for meals had recently been increased? Were they discontented because while the managers were allowed car parking space, the works force in general had to park their cars some way away from the entrance to the factory? Were they upset by my new directive on absenteeism?

"We listed fifteen possible causes, but still didn't feel that we had found the real cause.

"Then we thought of ten improbable causes, which included the machinations of a competitor to close us down, and a mole undermining all the good relationships we had had with the work force in the past.

"Over and over again we went through the names of the known left wingers in the shops – but our left wingers were only just left of centre, and we couldn't pinpoint anyone who would be able to build up some grievance to the extent that he would get the work force to consider a strike.

"We came to the conclusion that it must be the pay. But why, at that time?

"We carried out a benefit/risk analysis. Could we benefit from a strike at that time rather than later?

"We came to these conclusions:

1 the group's liquid resources were high
2 we could stand a two-months' strike without letting our customers down too badly
3 the management team could carry out some of the manufacturing processes
4 we could switch some of the manufacturing to our other factories
5 the work force would be hard hit after the third week. At that time they could claim tax rebates. They would, we determined, have to settle within four to six weeks at the most.

"Then followed the risk analysis:

1 there would be two big contracts that we couldn't fulfil, and these two customers might switch to our competitors, so long term we could lose heavily
2 the sales force would quickly become despondent trying to explain matters to irate customers, and we could lose good sales
3 if we switched to other factories it could become the first major strike in the whole Huntley group, and that would quickly deplete our resources
4 some of the managers might refuse to cross the picket lines
5 the publicity would be bad
6 even if we beat the strike there would be rancour for months ahead and it would be difficult to return to our previous happy relationship.

"The list was lengthy, and eventually we came to the conclusion that the risks outweighed any possible benefits of a strike at that time. Although I felt it might be better to take a tough stand, remember I was a new boy and if I caused an all-out strike it would be my head that would be on the block. A couple of days later Alan Todd called for an urgent meeting. We held it ten minutes later; Alan said he had some news for us. He had been in the sheet metal shop and had overheard Tim O'Malley, one of our loyalist supporters who had been with us twelve years or more, shouting that they must stand firm. He was insisting that 'they've made the biggest bloody profits ever and they ought to share them with us'.

"Todd explained that he had been hidden from most of the workers, and in any event, he was usually considered a non-person in the workshop, they had no time for accountants. As he had been out of sight behind the Trumph unit he had backed away as quickly as he could. He recalled that when we had been considering improbable causes we had thought there could possibly be a mole, although we couldn't pinpoint anyone. And certainly, we should never have considered that Tim O'Malley could be that mole.

"I won't bother you with all the details now, but Bob Denton quickly summed up the position: O'Malley was a moderate and had often fought the so-called left-wingers, but when the computerised bending and cutting machine was installed, instead of appointing him to be in charge, as everyone had expected, we gave Philps the job of chief supervisor. We believed mistakenly that the loyal O'Malley would understand that although he had only been with us two years, Philps had got the job because he had had previous experience with the Trumph computerised unit. O'Malley had given us the impression that he had accepted the situation, but evidently he had not.

"Subsequently we learned that O'Malley's attitude had changed almost overnight. He had gone to the trouble of obtaining a set of our accounts from Companies House and then began turning the minds of his fellow workers against us on the grounds that we were getting rich on their backs – a typical 'commie' statement, although O'Malley was nowhere near being a communist."

Manley paused, then said, "Of course, nowadays we go through the accounts with our works committee every year, and explain exactly what happens to our profits to ensure expansion and more job opportunities. But O'Malley had burrowed away, until eventually he was able to turn a very moderate work force into a most militant group."

"How did you solve it?" asked McAllister.

"Bob Denton saw O'Malley and offered him a senior post as foreman, and O'Malley was taken aback. Denton mentioned casually that that was why the junior post had been given to Philps. Well, there's nothing like promotion and more cash to change a man's mind. Bob, of course, pretended that he knew nothing about O'Malley's activities as a mole. He was careful to explain that he realised that O'Malley, as a loyal employee, would never be on the side of the militants, and strike or no strike, they had to consider the future – and that O'Malley was a part of that future. From then on it was easy. To help the works committee save their face we offered another one per cent to be effective six months later.

"It wasn't as simple as that! It entailed many, many hours of negotiation, but once we had won over O'Malley there was no real problem. Since then he's done a very good job for us and will soon be retiring, but if we had not considered all the improbable causes, would Alan have connected O'Malley with that unknown mole? Very doubtful!"

Everyone congratulated Bill on the splendid way he had so succinctly presented his case on problem solving.

"Let's talk some more about improbable causes," said McAllister; and this they did for some time. Finally McAllister said to the financial director, "OK, Larry – your turn."

Larry said, "I'm sorry, but I couldn't think of a good enough case study to highlight the basics of problem solving. I've had plenty of problems to solve, as my friends here know, but they all relate to some aspect of the financial affairs of the company."

"You should have told us earlier," said Lawson, "and we'd have thought one up for you."

Duckworth flushed angrily. "I don't need your help – I've told you the reason."

McAllister said, "There's no need for concern. It's my job to think of all eventualities, and it's always possible that someone may opt out of giving a case study – or that a case study wouldn't cover the fundamentals of problem solving, which is the object of the exercise. And forgive me for reminding everyone – as I shall continue to do at every meeting – that if leadership slips up it is often because fundamentals have been overlooked. Problem solving is important under the heading of *motivating leadership*, because it is the one way of invariably winning the respect of subordinates. When a subordinate sees a leader carrying out a problem solving exercise which results in a good solution, he is motivated to improve his own leadership qualities."

McAllister felt certain that Larry Duckworth had decided on his case study story, but having heard the brilliant expositions of Tom Lawson and Bill Manley had concluded that he didn't want to compete. He was sure that if this were not so, Larry would have explained the position at the beginning of the meeting. Black mark Larry!

He continued, "I'll give you a case history now that will bring out a feature so far not really covered. It is *creating ideas* to help solve a problem. It shows, too, how easy it is not to discover the true cause. This concerns one of the largest liners afloat, the 87,000 ton luxury liner the *USA*. It's a great ship, beautifully decorated and furnished to take in comfort some two thousand passengers, all first-class. Its objective is to compete with the *QEII* on the Atlantic run, as well as on world cruises. They have cruises out of Miami to the West Indies in October, November and December, crossing the Atlantic as well as cruising to Mediterranean ports during the summer, while the world cruises take place in January, February and March.

"The Managing Director of the line called us in when their head office in New York began receiving too many complaints, mostly through travel agents. We carried out an investigation over a six-week period – a most enjoyable assignment for our consultants. On their return we had our usual meeting, and these facts emerged: the captain was in complete charge of the ship, but his main concern was the safety of the vessel and general maritime affairs; the staff captain was mainly responsible for the crew; the chief purser controlled all the other ship's

activities; his deputy dealt mainly with the catering; the
third purser controlled the bureau dealing with passengers' day-to-day problems. There were also supervisors,
covering each of the decks, rooms and restaurants. The
controls were excellent, the executive staff competent.
There were the usual, inevitable, daily strings of complaints at the bureau, ranging from noisy cabins to sulky
stewards, but with two thousand passengers on board
these complaints, although not liked, were to be
expected, and everything was done to try and put things
right.

"But at head office they were receiving the more
serious complaints – letters written to travel agents
stating that the writers would never travel on the ship
again because . . . 'We were treated like cattle . . .' 'We
had to queue everywhere for everything . . .'

"Our first objective was to discover the cause of the
problem which we finally decided was poor communication. We held a brainstorming session. Question after
question was asked of the consultants, to try to find the
main factor. Comparisons were made of what *was*
happening with the *ideal* situation. Many solutions were
put forward but none seemed right. Then we began
tackling individual situations – for example, room
service. We wrote down as many as thirty ideas for
improvements. We brainstormed catering. Again, many
ideas were produced relevant to menus and the general
service.

"After two days of hard work which we thought should
cover our consultancy fee anyway, we had arrived at no
overall idea of why so many travellers should be so
disgruntled. None of the letters of complaint were
specific enough; they were all generalisations, the writers
setting out simply to condemn the ship. When contacted
for more specific reasons for complaints, they rarely
replied.

"We decided on a different approach. We checked for

details of every complaint received by travel agents and head office, and we would not be put off. We traced passengers and either called on them or telephoned. We ran them through a programmed computer to find a common denominator – and we found what we were seeking.

"All the major complaints seemed due to the fact that no one on the ship could give permission for a rule to be broken, or give instructions for extra expenditure which could nullify a complaint. As an example, when the ship stayed overnight in Southampton the crew expected leave. This meant evacuating the ship. The passengers who were due to remain on the ship for a cruise to other ports before returning to New York had to leave their cabins. They were, the company felt, being very fairly treated by being taken on a tour or a coach trip to London, where they stayed overnight. But the majority of the passengers were elderly. They did not want to be away from the ship – they didn't want to have to pack even a small bag for an overnight stay. However, when they queried this instruction while on board they were told that 'it was the rule because there was no staff remaining on the ship to look after them or even to provide a cold meal'!

"No one was able to authorise some of the crew to remain on board on overtime pay, to ensure that those passengers who wanted to stay on the ship could do so. This could have been arranged so easily, as we proved later to the company's executives. It was one of the complaints which had a wide ranging effect, sometimes deterring friends of the passengers from booking on the ship.

"Another complaint was having to queue for tour tickets while on board; sometimes, such queues could last an hour or more. No one complained at the time because it was 'the rule'. Subsequently, however, angry letters were sent to the ship's head office or a travel agent

– not necessarily complaining about the tours, but about queueing generally. No one considered it necessary for any changes to be made, because the ship's officers took queues for granted – it had always been like that.

"The solution was simple: tour tickets should be sold at the same time as cabins were booked. At that stage, passengers would be eager to book tours, and extra coaches could be laid on if necessary, and everyone accommodated. It would be more profitable for the company and would save queues on board. An easy problem to solve, but no one had previously been aware even that a problem existed.

"During one voyage to the Far East a violent storm with gale force winds destroyed a number of deckchairs. This, obviously, led to a shortage of chairs subsequently, but no one on board could give the order to purchase chairs at the next port of call. The captain was concerned over the ship's timetable, and the other officers were all concerned with their own specific duties. The chief purser, who, no doubt, would have liked to be able to purchase the chairs at a local port, had no authority to do so.

"Everything had to be reported to head office, and head office would then decide whether any action should be taken – and mostly, they decided to take no action, as it was too late anyway.

"Now, we discovered our mistake. So far we had not found the *true* cause – and the *true* cause was that no one on the ship had the authority to make a decision which might break a company rule, or entail the spending of company money to ensure the greater satisfaction of the passengers – and satisfied passengers breed more satisfied passengers . . .

"We pointed out that the company was spending huge sums of money on advertising, to motivate people to travel on the *USA*, and yet they were losing so many passengers through discontent. They were, of course, highly efficient executives at head office – otherwise they would never have called us in, would they? The solution we suggested was to appoint a managing director for the ship, with the authority that went with the position. When problems arose which needed instant decisions, he would make those decisions. When problems arose which needed instant expenditure, he would have the authority to sanction that expenditure.

"By considering improbable causes, but also by sifting through dozens of ideas, we solved the problem. On board ship they had been wont to think that the customer was always wrong. What was the harm in a little queueing, anyway? At headquarters they were too remote to understand the feelings of passengers who had paid a considerable sum of money to travel on the liner and wanted luxury service, all the way."

"That's a very good case study," said Fairley, "and one I can certainly use. I'm sure you can fill in a few more details for me."

"Of course," said McAllister.

Lawson said, "What was the result of the change in booking procedures for tours?"

"Believe it or not," said McAllister, "tour bookings went up by 25 per cent."

There followed further discussions on problem solving generally, then McAllister closed the meeting.

"You may or may not be pleased to hear," he concluded, "that at our next meeting Roland Huntley himself wishes to be present. He wants to talk about decision making, and the meeting is to be held in his apartment in Eaton Square."

9 Motivating Others to Make the Right Decision

.

Roland Huntley's apartment in Eaton Square comprised the ground floor and first floor of a building which had once housed the Earl of Michingham, his five children, and a retinue of ten staff. Roland's apartment was spacious enough to have a thirty-foot living room, a dining-room and a kitchen on the ground floor, and five bedrooms plus a library on the first floor – enough bedrooms for Roland, his wife Tessa, and their three children, who now only occasionally stayed at Eaton Square. Philip, aged forty, was living in New York with his third wife; Billy, aged twenty-eight and happily married, was farming in Australia; and Liza, thirty-five and divorced, lived in Monaco.

Daddy had provided well for all three children, with trust funds holding shares in the Huntley Group.

The Huntleys employed a husband-and-wife team, the husband acting as valet/chauffeur, while the wife organised the cleaning and cooking.

The meeting was being held in the dining-room, it being more spacious than the study. The centre piece was a beautiful eighteenth century mahogany table surrounded by matching chairs. On the walls were paintings – not in the category of Rubens, Rembrandt, or Matisse, but valued nevertheless at well over a million pounds. The table was covered with a baize cloth to protect its surface from the scratching of pens on notepads.

The four directors arrived together, as usual.
McAllister followed a few minutes later, at eight-fifty-five
am. The meeting was due to begin at nine.

The magic of Roland Huntley's personality worked,
even in his absence. The directors talked quietly while
they examined the paintings they had seen many times
before. The occasional laughter seemed forced.
McAllister knew that in every company there is a wide
gap between the chief executive and the board of
directors; although they may appear to be on the
friendliest of terms and at meetings they might disagree
and even argue strongly in support of their cause, the gap
was still unbridgeable.

First names were always used; wives were seemingly
on the warmest of terms with the chief executive's wife –
but this didn't alter the fact that the directors knew that
it was the chief executive who could decide their future,
at the press of a buzzer.

And that, thought McAllister, was the reason for the
totally unnatural atmosphere which so often preceded a
meeting of this kind. If they were more on edge on this
occasion, it was because the directors knew that soon – in
days, weeks, but not more than six months – Roland
Huntley would announce his most important decision:
the name of his successor as chief executive of the
Huntley Group.

Promptly at 9 am Huntley walked into the room and
shook hands with each of the men in turn. He then
insisted on McAllister taking the seat at the head of the
table and acting as chairman, while he placed himself
between Duckworth and Lawson. Manley and Fairley
sat opposite, leaving four empty chairs at the table.

"It's your show, Don," said Huntley.

"Thank you," responded McAllister, "and I call upon
you, Roland, to open the meeting on decision making."

They all looked expectantly at Huntley.

Iron grey hair, fashionably styled, a round face which

often wore an impish smile, grey/blue eyes which someone had once said were really X-rays, disguised as eyes, and an expressive mouth. Sometimes the lips were relaxed, warm and understanding; on other occasions when he was upset or antagonistic to an idea, they formed a fearsome straight line. When pursed, every aspect of an argument was being thrashed out in his computer mind. Now the lips were soft, and slightly parted in a smile, the eyes kindly.

Everyone relaxed a little. Huntley began, "Gentlemen, first I want to cover the arrangements made for your welfare. We shall not have the usual coffee breaks – they waste so much time and disturb the pattern of the meeting. I promise you a pleasant lunch, prepared by Howard because his wife is away at the moment. Incidentally, so is mine. I have arranged for lunch to be served early – at twelve noon – and we shall continue until tea at three-thirty, and close the meeting at four to four-thirty."

This means, thought Lawson, that the Old Man is either going to the theatre or an early dinner, otherwise he would have kept us here until two o'clock in the morning – by which time we should all be wilting, and he would still be going strong.

Roland continued, "We can work through lunch and tea, which will be served in here. There are two lavatories on this floor – one adjacent to the entrance, and the other at the end of the corridor."

Fairley thought, we've all been here before but he still has to spell everything out!

"I have given instructions," Huntley went on, "that we are not to be disturbed by telephone calls. Don has written up the notes of previous meetings, which have been distributed. Any comments?"

Nobody replied, so Huntley continued, "On this occasion I have set up a recorder which I shall now switch on."

McAllister sighed. They had all agreed at the first meeting that recordings inhibited free speech, and that only the salient features would be noted by McAllister.

After checking that the recorder was working satisfactorily Huntley continued, "I understand that previous meetings have gone extremely well and I am sure the same will apply to-day." Pausing, he smiled at each man in turn, then said, "You will have wondered why I asked to be present at this meeting. There are two reasons: I disagree with the nonsense suggested by Don that my presence might cause unnecessary tension. That, as you all know, is quite ridiculous. We hold board meetings every month, and there are no tensions – neither has my presence prevented free speech. They are, in my opinion, models of what board meetings should be. I am sure you will agree with that."

They didn't, but they all nodded, just the same.

"Don, I wanted to prove to you that I am no dictator," Huntley said, "and that my board would not stand for it if I were. I wanted to vindicate myself in your eyes, and that is one reason why I am here."

There was amusement in McAllister's eyes, but he decided not to comment. After all, Huntley was the paymaster! He thought it best not to emphasise that chief executives always have inhibiting factors at every meeting. He didn't think, for example, that Huntley would have appreciated Manley's statement that he – Huntley – often acted unfairly. There could have been no debate on that subject if the chief executive had been present on that occasion.

He heard Huntley asking, "Are you happy about that, Don?"

"Of course; I only raised the point in the first place because of my experience of such meetings – but experience need not always be a guideline on every occasion."

"Well put, Don," said Huntley. "My second reason is

that I believe the most important feature in successful leadership is making the right decisions. Our board meetings are all about decision making – should we do this, should we do that, should we spend or cut . . . And if you will all forgive me for saying so, I consider that I know more about the rights and wrongs of decision making than most leaders. That is why I thought my contribution would be valuable to you."

Tom Lawson said, "You're right, Roland, let's not beat about the bush. We have all agreed time and time again that you have a knack of getting to the heart of the matter; you always seem to know when there is a cover-up; generalisations are anathema to you; you ignore non-facts and you make the right decisions. If we, as a board, maintain that standard, it is mainly thanks to your guidance, and as for your being here, we all welcome it!"

Bill Manley thought Lawson was sucking up a bit – but then, he always did in Manley's eyes.

"Thank you, Tom," said Huntley. "I am sure you are all going to discuss every aspect of decision making, and I don't intend to interfere. I shall let each discussion run its course – but you're the chairman, Don, and if I do speak out of turn, or go on too long, you must pull me up. I shall respect your judgement. I want to touch on computer involvement in problem solving and decision making – also on factual evidence and emotional involvement."

Which just about covers the lot, thought Fairley.

"I shall begin by stating that problem solving and decision making go together like birds of a feather, or sap in a tree – there can't be one without the other. Let us look at it in its simplest form; when we are about to decide on a holiday there is a problem – shall we stay here or shall we go abroad? This calls for a solution, and the solution leads to a decision. If we have all decided long ago where we are holidaying, then there is no decision to make and no facts or brochures to obtain. But if there are conflicting views, there is a problem, and someone has to make the final decision.

"If there is a breakdown of machinery, first comes the problem solving by craftsmen or engineers, or research personnel – then the decision is based on information. Should the machinery be repaired in a simple manner, or in a more sophisticated way, but at a higher cost? If the first option is taken up, do we risk further breakdowns? Or should the machinery be replaced altogether? If not, should we hold large stocks of spare parts in case of future breakdowns and in order to facilitate speedy repairs? I can't think of any decision which is not preceded by a problem. Can anyone here think of one?"

Lawson said, "When, recently, we took over Grant Brothers, that decision, surely, did not arise out of any problem."

"It most certainly did!" Huntley broke in. "They were small competitors. The problem was, could they become big competitors, and give us headaches at some time in the future? To solve the problem we could have let things slide, believing that they were not efficient and they might, therefore, fail anyway, or their price-cutting could lead to bankruptcy; or could we have started an even more severe price cutting war in an attempt to close them down? Or should we buy them out? When we had evaluated all the facts we decided to buy. That was a decision arising out of alternatives."

Lawson said, "Fair enough! But let me give you another example: when I decide with a regional director to increase the sales promotion budget, it isn't because we have a problem."

"You're wrong, Tom. There are two reasons why you agree to increase expenditure: because you have had previous problems in not obtaining a high enough return on sales; or because you consider that such a problem might arise in the future. You evaluate the problems and come to the decision to spend more money."

Lawson laughed. "You win, Roland!"

The chief executive's lips tightened. "It isn't a case of winning, Tom, it's a question of logic prevailing. But we need not continue on these lines.

"So the decision maker, in the first place, usually relies on other people to provide him with alternative solutions, or the information necessary for him to arrive at a decision. If he is a one-man business, he has to solve the problem for himself, and make the decision. It is the problem solver, however, who provides all the ammunition necessary for the decision maker to fire his guns successfully."

A shocking analogy, thought Duckworth, but Huntley, not being able to read minds, continued, "Now we come to a vital point in decision making, and I am making two categorical statements: first, too many decisions are made without studying all the information and analysing all the facts provided; and secondly, that the decision maker too often makes up his mind on a line of action in spite of the facts which have emerged, and which should have changed his thinking. I shall give you two examples. In the first, three hundred redundancies were called for by a managing director because costs had to be cut. Facts showed that a hundred and sixty should be the maximum, for if an expected upturn in the economy occurred, supplies to customers would be in jeopardy through lack of craftsmen. But the managing director ignored these facts. He was more concerned with the reactions of the City to half-hearted decisions on his part, and he insisted, therefore, on the three hundred redundancies. That decision was made in spite of the facts, and it proved to be a wrong one.

"In case number two, facts proved that a sales department situated at a factory in Suffolk should be moved to the company's headquarters in London. All the facts showed that the move was correct, but the managing director did not want to overcrowd his London headquarters. To him it was a personal matter. He decided to make a good case for the retention of the sales department at the factory. Status quo won the day; the facts were not accepted by the managing director, and he made the wrong decision.

"The next question we must ask ourselves is: why are the full facts not always called for? Why do some executives believe in standard generalisations such as 'everyone knows . . . all the staff agree . . . there's no alternative if we are to increase exports . . .'? The answer to both the case studies I gave you, as well as the generalisations, is in some personal or emotional involvement. You have all, at times, asked me for decisions, when you only wanted me to agree with you because you had become personally or emotionally involved in a project.

"Larry, for example, can't ever spend enough on computers, because there is always a computer which supersedes and revolutionises everything, and will enable the staff numbers to be cut – although this rarely happens. Larry is normally clinically minded – a logical thinker – and his mind is only clouded when he is personally involved in a new computer project.

"When Larry is tunnel-minded he provides me with the facts as he sees them. If I insist on making my own enquiries I am being difficult, and obstructing development. There always has to be a speedy decision if we are to get delivery, or a price advantage . . . Forgive me, Larry, and don't blame yourself – I am the same, in other directions.

"Now for you, Tom. Last year you wanted to hold the greatest ever convention – not in London, but in Honolulu. And Tom, you were so emotionally involved in the project, so enthusiastic, that you couldn't believe that there could be any alternative. You kept telling me that our standing in the eyes of the world would be jeopardised, and in the eyes of our buyers and distributors, if we did not have an outstanding conference which, for some reason, had to be held in Honolulu. Wrong decisions due to personal involvements go right down the line. If a secretary has set her heart on a new type of electronic typewriter, then no logic will change her mind. No car lover should ever be allowed to make a decision regarding a company's car policy. No gourmet should ever decide on what is, and what is not, justifiable for entertaining expenses. You may ask, what is the difference between enthusiasm and emotional involvement. Very little! I am not saying that when someone is involved in a decision making process, he is always wrong. Not at all! He may more often be right than wrong. But why take a fifty-fifty chance? Why not base judgements on facts? No one has ever gone bankrupt through basing decisions on facts.

"That is why a managing director must always be a *NO* man when asked for a decision by an enthusiast or someone emotionally involved. They could both be right, but both should be made to prove why they are right. Neither will have considered all the facts. They will have brushed aside queries from associates or subordinates. The *NO* man, when faced with this problem, will look impassive, listen carefully and will consider positives and negatives – benefits and risks. He will then insist that the person involved should prove his points step by step, fact by fact, that his claims are justified. The *NO* man slows down the whole decision making process so that the truth can emerge. This, of course, means continual battles of the type that I have so often had with enthusiasts and those emotionally involved, when decision making.

"Forgive me if I again repeat this most important point: more bad decisions are made through personal involvement, often related to new ideas, or more usually to additional expenditure, than from any other factor in decision making. It makes hard-headed men soft-headed, weak men hysterical and rational men irrational.

"My next point is concerned with the use of computers in decision making. Computers, I have been told, take away the risk element. They don't. What they do is to prove rapidly whether facts are correct or not, and offer alternative solutions. They show up weaknesses against a known profile, and provide every conceivable type of data in a matter of possibly seconds. The difference between computers and manual effort is only speed. Given enough time and talent, all the information churned out by a computer, whether it be concerned with a flight to the moon or the treatment of disease, could be worked out by manpower. The computer only provides alternative solutions or data on which a decision can be based. It doesn't make the decision, unless, of course, programmed by humans to do so. This applies to so many aspects in the technical, biological, and mechanical fields: for example, a computer can be programmed to instigate immediate action if there should be an oxygen failure in a space ship, by causing a reserve supply to be switched on. But these decisions by computers have to be programmed in by people – the computer acts on human instructions.

"You may think this comes under the heading of useless information because it is so well known. Why, therefore, am I talking at such length on this subject?"

All four directors had already been wondering why – they were all fully conversant with the operation of computers.

"It is because," went on Huntley, "I am tired of hearing that the computer has made a statement, or the computer keeps the stocks at the right level . . . the right level is decided by an employee and if he gets it wrong, the computer gets it wrong. We must have facts on which to base our decisions, but we must not make the mistake of demanding useless information from a computer.

"Tom Lawson once showed me a print-out of a day's

work by a salesman. Tom was bubbling with enthusiasm; everything, he told me, was there except the weather report. Now he knows that too much was being asked of the computer – too much unnecessary information was printed out.

"We are living in a fantastic, computerised age, and my advice to you is to remember that you make the decisions – not the computer."

With that, to everyone's surprise, Huntley said, "That's all for the moment."

Duckworth knew quite well what the computer talk was all about. It was another aspect of decision making; a warning to him not to go ahead with the new plan for further expansion of the computer system without a great deal more thought. Huntley was conditioning everyone for a decision which might go against the main board's general vote. It was, Duckworth knew, one of Huntley's techniques to implant in the minds of others thoughts of a decision which might soon have to be made. He was influencing minds, and doing it so cleverly; was that the reason why he had wanted to attend this meeting? Duckworth thought it was, and he knew that he had to regain some authority.

"May I give you my viewpoint on the subject?" he said.

Huntley said, "Well, there's not much point –" But McAllister interrupted, "Yes, Larry – go ahead."

Duckworth said, "I agree that the computer doesn't make the decisions unless programmed to do so, but it does demand the acceptance of the 'what if –' principle – a means of visualising future possibilities and probabilities. A computer will provide logical conclusions which enable us to make what you, Roland, often term calculated decision making.

"Another factor is that at some time or other, most employees indulge in cover-ups – the truth is hidden, which means problems for decision makers. There can be manufacturing faults, service breakdowns, customer complaints . . . and these cover-ups could all lead to a series of wrong decisions, if it weren't for the computer. A computer can pinpoint the problem areas, by the very questions asked of it, and the answers given ensure that a cover-up will be uncovered.

"Also, in the pre-computer days there were too many snap decisions made. Fifty per cent could be right – fifty per cent could be wrong. With the computer providing constant information we are now ninety per cent right most of the time. Just think of our management accounts. Until a few years ago we used to receive them, at best, four weeks after the close of a period. Now we get them one day after the period ends. Think what that means for decision making! Stock control decisions, too, are now made on a day-to-day basis; we know exactly what our requirements will be one, two, even six months ahead. It is my aim to improve continually on this system and, by so doing, improve our decision making."

McAllister held up his hand. "You've convinced us – but we didn't need convincing that computers are essential to decision making."

Duckworth said wryly, "But all along you have insisted that we must get back to fundamentals, and I have been covering fundamentals."

Duckworth knew that he, on his part, was endeavouring to influence his fellow directors to side with him when the question of changing the computer system was raised at a board meeting.

"I can't see the relevance of all this," interrupted Huntley. "Aren't we supposed to be discussing motivating leadership, and how, by good decision making, we can motivate others?"

Typical of our Roland! thought Manley. He started the discussion by almost accusing Duckworth of spending money recklessly on new computer systems. Now that he suspects he might be losing out, he accuses Duckworth of getting away from the issue.

Unperturbed by the interruption Duckworth said, "I do want to make one more point." He knew that, indirectly, he was fighting for a future decision in his favour. "When Tom was planning the introduction of our new all-purpose extinguisher we set up a mathematical model to cover the relationship between sales and profits. We wanted accurate predictions. We set up the control so that we could make instant decisions to change the policies where necessary. Sales promotion expenses were accurately forecast at each stage of the launch. The model identified many factors, and we had a flow chart covering the variables. Tom will agree that the model enabled us to make the correct decisions at each stage, and the result was the most successful launch within the history of Huntley's. I can cite many more cases of the effectiveness of computers in decision making, but I'd like to make a final point."

"Not another final point," Manley exploded.

"Well, another point then. You don't need me to tell you, Roland, that you are an entrepreneurial genius. You have made decisions without the use of computer predictions, and because you are you, they have nearly always been right. But you can't expect that kind of experience from lesser men, and for that reason alone, I believe we should set up a special computer training division so that if – and when – our new computer centre is opened, our under managers will know how they can make full use of it, in their decision making."

Huntley, who at one time had felt his temper rising, was completely mollified, and Fairley thought that Duckworth had presented his case brilliantly.

Huntley said with a laugh, "All right, Larry, we'll talk about your project again later. Now can we get on with other decision making processes?"

McAllister said, "Roland has emphasised that decisions must be based on factual evidence. Larry has said that such evidence is often best arrived at by the use of computers. I should like to make the point now that even facts can be suspect. We all know that computer errors can occur; therefore, if a computer shows a wide discrepancy between what is forecast and what managers believe is possible, don't believe the computer. Also, to re-emphasise another point, look behind the facts if you believe that someone emotionally involved could have manipulated those facts to suit his or her purpose. That is something else that can be done by computers!

"Now, let us discuss other points of view on decision making. It's your turn, Bill."

Bill said, "I'd like to talk about computers . . ."

Everyone laughed, and this relaxed the atmosphere, which had become tense while Huntley was attacking Duckworth and Duckworth was responding.

Manley said, "I believe that a major factor in decision making is the fear that many managers have over making decisions. A high risk solution might be correct, but some managers will always go for the low risk solution, for fear of repercussions. And this applies quite often when technical decisions have to be made. When managers have drummed into them, as I may say our managers have, the need to cut costs, they can make incorrect decisions. Maybe it's a failure of my – or should I say our – leadership, that too often the soft option is adopted, because of fear of repercussions. Now that leadership strengths and weaknesses are being brought into the open we ought to consider this aspect. When I first joined the company there was a boom on and the mood was 'safety last'. But since then it has become 'safety first' – not only in our group, but in other leading companies throughout the world. Have we gone too far over to safety first in decision making?"

Huntley said, "Bill, safety first is always right when it is not known how long an economic depression may last, but decisions change. What could have been correct five years ago could be wrong to-day, and what is right now could have been a bad decision five years ago."

"I'm not criticising you, Roland, I'm only stating a fact. Managers are, too often, scared to make decisions. If a joking innuendo is made – 'if it goes wrong it's you for the chop!' or, 'he'll have your guts for garters' – or some similar remark, that could have a devastating effect on middle management and could lead to bad decisions."

"I'm sure," said Huntley, "that none of you have been frightened to make decisions because of my influence on you; but I can see that great care must be taken in the future not to use implied threats when decisions are called for, and risks have to be taken. Don was, obviously, right. Our leadership hasn't been good enough!"

Manley said, with a wry look at Huntley, "That's a good point. We have to take the fear out of decision making." But Huntley didn't get the message, although all the other directors did. "When asked for decisions our thinking is sometimes coloured by whether we like someone or not. I can quote many bad decisions made by managers who knew they were wrong, but could not bear to think they were agreeing with an associate or subordinate they disliked."

He paused, and Fairley interrupted, "Bill, what you are referring to is the *halo* effect. We are all apt to agree with those we admire and disagree with those we don't like. This can certainly lead to bad decision making. You are right, Bill, we have to emphasise that leadership means listening carefully to all pleadings – whether they come from obnoxious people or most agreeable people – and the more we dislike someone, the more carefully we ought to listen to them before coming to a decision."

Manley said drily, "I do know of the *halo* effect, Hugh, and was about to mention it when you interrupted."

"Sorry, Bill," said Hugh apologetically.

"Apology accepted," said Manley, without a smile.

Then, "I also believe that a decision should be changed if new evidence provides a reason for the change. Too often a decision maker stands by his decision because he doesn't want to admit that he was at fault, or that he had not considered every eventuality. This applies particularly to middle managers, whose subordinates may suggest improvements which could mean overriding the manager's previous decision."

"And how do you overcome that personality trait?" asked Duckworth.

Manley answered, "By encouraging more group decision making. This has been tried in our factories in Germany and Norway and has worked well. Managers here – and especially directors – arrive at decisions without consultation. I find it almost impossible in this country to motivate directors and managers to consult with subordinates before important decisions are made, and to convince them that that need not delay decision making. The problem is – especially with regional managers – that they believe it is their right to make all decisions. They feel it undermines their authority if they ask the opinions of others."

Huntley said, "I know you are not implying that I come to decisions without consulting you."

"Well, you do sometimes," said Manley bravely. "Often, the first I hear about a decision is after I return from an overseas trip and find that the decision was made in my absence."

"Are you suggesting, then, that business must stand still while you are away?"

Manley knew he couldn't win, so he said, "I've overstepped the mark again, trying to prove my case. But as I said before, obviously there are occasions when instant decisions have to be made and you, Roland, do, most of the time, consult us."

Roland said, "Good! But I do agree that there should be more consultation at middle management level, with the proviso that this must not delay action. Over and over again, as you know, we have made quick decisions and have won victories while our competitors were holding meeting after meeting before deciding on what action to take."

Manley felt that he had made the right impression as a tough executive who was still willing to see the viewpoint of others. He was confident that Huntley would appreciate his direct speaking.

"Thank you, Bill," said McAllister. "Now it's your turn, Hugh."

Fairley began, "I want to take up a point raised by Bill. It needs emphasising that too many bad decisions are made because A dislikes B, so that whenever B suggests anything, A automatically vetoes it – and vice versa. Good decision making then becomes almost impossible. We ought to take this matter up very strongly at managing director level, and emphasise that all managers must be more objective when making decisions."

Huntley said, "Any executive with us whose decisions are affected by his likes or dislikes should be sacked; and if that isn't possible he should be bought off. I can honestly say that I have never allowed personal feelings to affect any of my decisions."

Hugh said, "We all know that, Roland. Shall I continue?"

"Please do," said Huntley, forgetting that McAllister was chairman of the meeting.

Hugh said, "I want to give six decision making principles that we outline at our courses. I don't believe there is anything wrong with our teaching, but I now realise that we make the mistake of not ensuring subsequently that our teachings are carried out. Here are the six principles:

"One – Gather all the information.
"Two – Examine all the alternative actions which

could be taken when the information has been provided.

"Three – Analyse all possible consequences of these actions.

"Four – Having identified the consequences, place in order the probability of these consequences occurring – computers should be used at this stage.

"Five – Determine the most desirable alternative – the one where the probability of risk is low and the probability of success high.

"Six – Make the decision on all the evidence provided.

"Throughout our analysis we use possibly the best of all decision making principles, summed up in the words *what if* . . . These were mentioned earlier by Larry. The technique is as old as the hills, but is rarely used – especially if the decision maker is, himself, involved in the project – if it is his innovation, or his design. It is never used by those executives who make up their minds too quickly, nor by those who like to play God and make all the decisions without consultation. We play what we call the *what if* . . . game during our courses, and put forward a number of decisions to the delegates, and then use the *what if* . . . principle: *What if we don't complete on time?* – the answer: *We have to pay compensation . . . What if we can't afford to pay the compensation? – We have to borrow the money . . . What if the bank won't loan us the money at that time?* . . . And so we continue.

"It's so simple, so old hat – but so rarely used. And it can be crucial to the decision making process. It's a fundamental – and we must, again, remind ourselves of these fundamentals.

"That is my contribution at the moment."

As he finished there came a discreet knock on the door, and Howard arrived to whisper in Huntley's ear that lunch was ready. And lunch was served, each of them receiving as a first course a small portion of rather unripe melon. After they had made a pretence of enjoying the

melon, they were served with the next course – two strips
of dry, slightly curling ham, and a slice of turkey, plus a
little potato salad. This was followed by coffee.

It was certainly the worst meal so far, Lawson thought
– but that's why he's rich and I'm poor.

Lunch over in less than thirty minutes, there was a
short break, and then the meeting resumed.

It was Tom Lawson's turn, and he said, "I want to refer
back to risk analysis. For this, I use a numbered system
to take away the guesswork. Simply, it entails a sheet of
paper divided into four columns. In the first column is
Risk A – for example, a possible strike. The marking is
from one to ten, and if I don't think there is a strong
possibility of a strike the number entered in this column
might be four.

"The second column is headed Risk B: if, because of a
go-slow, we can't deliver on time, compensation
payments will have to be made to the buyer. This is a
high risk, and I mark it nine.

"Risk C could be a failure in quality control due to
pressure on the work force to increase output – a pressure
which they might find unacceptable. The risk of
inefficient quality control might be marked at six.

"Risk D is the actual loss of the customer through
inability to complete or maintain quality. That is not
high, so I mark it four.

"The decision, now, is clear cut. Do we accept the
buyer's terms to deliver by a specified time, or do we ask
to be excused from quoting in this instance, because the
subsequent risks are too high?

"My decision is now made simple: total marks, 40.
Under fifty per cent marks – in this case, twenty – and
the risk is acceptable. Over fifty per cent, it is
unacceptable. The marking was 23 so in this case – and
Bill knows it was based on delivery of trucks to Kuwait –
the decision was that the risk was too great, and we told

our work force that we were refusing the order. The next day we had a deputation from the Works Committee assuring us of continual working on *our* conditions if the order was accepted. We accepted, and the orders were delivered on time and all was well.

"Although as marketing director I was influenced by wanting to get the order, I relied on the markings. You may say that all that was needed was common sense, but it was the markings that concentrated our minds, and it was showing these markings to the works force which undoubtedly influenced them. It's just another check on decision making. I have given a simple example, but it can be far more complicated than that.

"My next point involves all of our decision makers, from shop floor supervisors up to general management. Chief executives can make decisions from information which is not obtainable – or if obtainable, is not willingly given – to those who are half-way down the ladder. We have to ask ourselves whether our decision makers receive all the help and advice necessary from the higher echelon of management. Does red tape and office bureaucracy hinder decision making? Too many forms to complete, too many sanctions required; so that in the end the decision maker takes the easy way out, makes a decision without the necessary information – and it could be the wrong decision. Can overworked and frustrated managers be good decision makers in these circumstances? We on the main board, at the touch of a switch, the press of a buzzer, can get all the co-operation we want. If we took a census amongst our managers we should hear the same old excuses – 'When I have the time . . .' 'I haven't enough staff to cope . . .' 'The computer is already overworked . . .' 'Check with So-and-so . . .' We really do need to lay down some form of guidelines on decision making so that they can get all the information they require instead of coming up against this resistance."

"We do seem to be an inefficient group," said Huntley.

"Not at all," said Lawson. "They are a highly efficient group of managers, and compared with many other companies they receive tremendous backing – but as we are going back to fundamentals I feel that the matter should, again, be reviewed."

"I agree," said Huntley. "I also agree that we can be more efficient."

"But you are an efficient group," said McAllister, "I can assure you of that."

"Maybe," said Huntley, "but I'd like to ask you, Don, for your comments on the decision making processes."

"Sure, I'm glad to be able to come in on one of my favourite subjects. After all, if it weren't for bad decisions somewhere along the line, consultants wouldn't be needed. There are points I should like to make: the first is that almost always, decision making involves people, and decision makers sometimes overlook that decisions can prove to be wrong only because the human factor has been overlooked. So here are some pertinent questions to ask yourselves; will a decision so affect people that there could be repercussions? Are the people competent enough to carry out the decisions? Does all the information come from reliable people? Are the decision makers themselves competent enough to make the decisions? If negotiating, are you negotiating with the right people – the decision makers? Many managers pretend they can make decisions when they don't really have the authority. Can anyone undermine decisions which have been made? What type of people is involved in the decision making – moody, cheerful, enthusiastic, pessimistic, lazy . . . ?

"Personality traits can affect a decision's success or failure. Too many decision makers use such expressions as: 'Oh, she'll do it all right!' – she may not want to do it: 'He'll love it!' – he may hate it! or 'If they know what's good for them, they'll agree!' – they may not know what's good for them, and they may disagree.

"I have had several experiences where decision makers have told me that So-and-so will do this or that – and then have subsequently discovered that So-and-so was not at all keen, and objected to doing this and that. People are not always predictable, and managers are often not perceptive enough and judge others by their own standards.

"It is so important in decision making for managers to be able to assess people and their qualities. Always consider people when making a decision.

"Hugh has given us the principles for decision making now taught at your training centre. May I now give you *our* principles which are very similar, but with a slight difference of emphasis. More simply, they are a little Americanised. The mnemonic we use for decision making is the word *TARGET*, because you have to be on target to make the right decisions.

"*T* stands for *target* – what we aim to do; what we want to put right. It symbolises what we are seeking. What achievement are we aiming for? Is our target some form of improvement in design or production?

"*A* stands for *assessing the situation* – what do we need to hit the bullseye? Do we have the resources in cash or manpower to achieve the target? Can we acquire all the materials needed? Could there be a logistic problem? There must be a complete analysis covering every eventuality which could include wars, slumps, booms, stocks rising or falling, shipping problems . . .

"*R* stands for *reviewing the alternatives*. We now list the alternatives from all the assessments and information available, and we settle on the most favourable alternative.

"*G* stands for *get it right*. We review our choice. Does that choice provide the maximum benefit with the minimum risk?

"*E* stands for *evidence*. Like the counsel for the

defence, or the prosecution, we must provide all the evidence available to convince the chief executive, the plant manager, the designer, the export director who, possibly, has to confirm our decision.

"Except for the Roland Huntleys of this world, we always have to convince someone above us that we have made the right decision in the first place. We must be one hundred per cent committed to that decision and prepare our case very carefully. There must be no 'ifs' or 'buts' – no 'on this hand' or 'on that hand . . .' The executive concerned does not want us to sit on the fence. He wants a decision from us, so that he can either confirm or disagree with it. If we haven't got it right at this stage, then we must go through the whole exercise again.

"*T* now stands for *task completed*. Having made the decision we set up a series of check points so that at each stage we are certain that the decision is being correctly implemented. If our monitoring system is wrong, we risk failure. Now how about that?"

Huntley said, "Are you looking for praise, or criticism?"

"Only praise, please."

"Well, *TARGET* seems a good way to set out the principles, and I am sure Hugh will consider this when reviewing our courses."

"Thank you," said McAllister. "I think we have covered the ground adequately, but perhaps Roland will have the final word. How do you, Roland, make your decisions? What formula do you use?"

Huntley straightened his back, looked pleased at the request, and said, "If there has to be a difference between top executive and middle management, it could be that the experience of the top executive is such that his mind, storing all the knowledge he has acquired, automatically uses set principles whether it be for a sales presentation or decision making, without being conscious of the fact. Middle management, however, perhaps have to remind themselves of these fundamentals, although in turn, they are able to react automatically to some situations. Therefore, I am sure that, subconsciously, I use all your principles. The mind has to be correctly programmed – and that should be the objective behind every teaching session.

"There is little more I can add. Decision making has been very well covered. I know that you believe that on occasion, I am repetitious – but that is only to make sure that there can be no misunderstanding. To-day, however, it would be foolish to attempt to go over the ground which you have covered so adequately.

"There are many occasions when I am asked for a decision and I ask for time to make up my mind. For example, Mr X rushes in complaining that there is no possibility of working any longer with Executive Y, and Y must be moved. Or another enthusiastic arrival will tell me that I shall miss the boat unless I decide that minute to do this or that – the purchase of this plant, the addition of that factory . . .

"In many of these instances I, metaphorically speaking, put the problem and the decision into a drawer and forget it. Usually, when I look in the drawer again three weeks or three months later, I find that there is no need for a decision. X has made it up with Y, or there has been a slight drop in turnover and the extension is not urgently needed, or there was some miscalculating regarding the company we should have taken over . . . No one troubles to remind me that he or she even made the request.

"My advice is that decisions of great moment must be made at once. The lesser decisions can often be held a while in abeyance, and the problem goes away. And that's all."

"Thank you," said McAllister. "Before we close, I should like to talk for a moment about the subject for the next meeting. It is, as you know, about negotiating. I have a friend staying with us at the moment – Craig Nelson. Maybe the name is not very familiar to you but he is a leading theatrical agent in Hollywood. He is also agent for many authors. Before he entered the film world he was connected with the oil industry. He negotiated for the film which was based on the oil industry, with Film Dynamics. He has spent his whole life negotiating, and he gives a series of seminars on the subject. It was after the oil film was made that he became one hundred per cent involved with the film industry.

"If you would like Craig to talk to us on negotiating, as a change from the standard formula of our meetings, I know he would be pleased to do so. He's a great fellow – you'd like him, and if you can negotiate with film stars and film directors you can negotiate anything."

The vote in favour was unanimous. The meeting closed at three-thirty, and it had been decided that the next meeting would be hosted by Larry Duckworth.

10   Negotiating and Motivating

Larry Duckworth's wife Angela considered herself a good business woman – but unlucky. She had opened a wool shop – intended to be the forerunner of a string of such shops, but as the first one never made any profits (not, of course, due to any fault of hers) the idea of becoming a chain shop owner was discarded. Then she progressed into home sales with morning coffee meetings where friends were invited to look at a range of chinaware. The parties were all great successes – except that very few people bought any chinaware. She backed out of that, explaining to Larry that she didn't want to continue entertaining people she didn't very much like. Next came perfumes she supplied by mail. The main beneficiaries of that business were the postal authorities. Her latest drive to become a business tycoon was buying and selling antique furniture, and advising on interior decorating. This, like all the other ventures, lost money – but husband Larry couldn't complain because it was her own inheritance money that she lost. She was now busily refurnishing and redecorating their new home in Islington – once a working class district but an area fast becoming a centre for artists and business people wanting to live near town without paying top property prices.

Larry's house, a four-storey building, was just right if one felt it was healthy to climb stairs continually. But to Angela it was a challenge; there were so many rooms to be filled with antique furniture and ceramics.

She had decided that the directors' meeting should be held in the living room, although Larry pointed out that the antique chairs there were not meant for long-term comfortable sitting.

Since they had been married some eighteen years earlier, Larry had had a series of affairs, always with teenage lovelies. His latest was a nineteen-year-old model, on whom he lavished both affection and gifts. Angela was completely unaware of Larry's affairs; she could not really visualise her rather dull, middle-aged husband, whose only hobby was work, having another interest chasing young girls. His affairs were discovered by chance when Tom Lawson and Roland Huntley, due to a flight cancellation, arrived unexpectedly at an hotel where a Mr & Mrs Smith were booked in only to find that this Mr & Mrs Smith were the company's financial director and his girlfriend.

Roland had agreed with Tom that Duckworth's affairs were of no concern to them, and it was best to keep his peccadilloes to themselves. But Tom knew that Roland would not forget. He would take Duckworth's affairs into consideration when deciding on his new chief executive.

The first to arrive at the meeting were Don McAllister and Craig Nelson. Nelson admired the antiques, to Angela's delight, especially as he gave the impression of being an authority on antique furniture. But if Angela had shown Nelson butterflies, neatly pinned to a board, she would still have thought him an authority. He was that kind of person.

Slow of speech, a thoughtful look as he contemplated a reproduction Sheraton desk, a wrinkled brow as he gazed intently at a map of London circa 1450 – all created an impression of great knowledge. Nelson, however, had been a failure academically, although later in life he had made up for this by becoming deeply interested in all forms of research. Every project he engaged in was studied in depth, so that he could, if necessary, disprove the statements of others, thus enhancing his own claims and reputation.

His foresight when in the oil industry enabled him to make a fortune quickly, but this wealth was just as quickly lost when he became involved with Hollywood. The glamour of the film world dulled his perceptions, and his ability to analyse facts. He invested most of his wealth in a film epic exposing the negotiating chicanery of oil men in Middle East countries, and the operations of the oil Mafia. The film, however, was panned by the critics, and filmgoers stayed away in their thousands.

Following the film failure, Craig helped out a friend – a manager/agent for actors and film stars. His analysis of that situation showed that there was room for a much larger organisation to safeguard the interests of, and to make fortunes for, stars in every artistic field. He opened his own agency, and within five years had become the most successful agent of all time. Leading actors and second billing actresses fought to get on his books, because he always negotiated and won top packages.

He and Don McAllister's father were the same age – both sixty-five – and they met when McAllister senior was carrying out an assignment in the oil industry. A friendship developed, and both men were now household names – McAllister in consultancy, Nelson in the film world.

Angela was delighted to listen to him expounding the gossip from Hollywood, and by the time the four directors had arrived, she was looking starry-eyed at Craig. Never before had she met such a kindly and understanding person, who seemed to know so much about everything and everybody.

There was no need for introductions, because McAllister had taken Nelson to headquarters a couple of days earlier, to enable him better to understand the negotiating activities of the group managers; and the directors had all previously met Angela. Three of them thought her an ideal wife for Larry Duckworth. Tom Lawson was not so sure.

They sat in chairs which might have been right for back sufferers, but were most uncomfortable for long-term seated sessions.

After Angela smiled her way out to prepare lunch, they relaxed, chatting for a moment, until McAllister opened the meeting by explaining that Craig Nelson had agreed that negotiating was an integral part of salesmanship, and had suggested that Tom Lawson should first explain the relationship. Craig and Tom had spent some time together working out their presentations, so that there would be no conflict.

McAllister continued, "Craig cannot understand why four top executives should have to listen to an explanation of the relationship between selling and negotiating. But I think I have convinced him that it was our determination to get back to fundamentals to enable us to assess the future training needs of our management staff as well as the better conduct of our own affairs. Now over to you, Tom."

Lawson began, "One word sums up the difference between selling and negotiating, and that word is *concessions*. The 'concession' stage is only reached, however, after the completion of some eighty-five per cent of the selling. Unfortunately, too many people – especially sales engineers, technicians and financial people – although all appreciating that from time to time they do negotiate, if only over the price of a house, do not believe that they are in any way concerned with salesmanship.

"Selling is simply influencing the mind of others, and this we attempt to do at all stages of negotiation. The difference, however, between the professional salesman and the non-believer is that professional salesmen work to a set plan while the non-believer does so more by chance than through planning.

"You, Bill, a great technician, maintain that you are, first and foremost, a production man and in no way involved in salesmanship. Yet I know you keep to the principles of salesmanship every time you negotiate – otherwise you would never have been so successful. You, Hugh, are selling, or influencing minds, almost daily when, for example, you are trying to convince a trade union official that he ought to agree to a compromise. First, the mind has to be conditioned – and only then can the concessions be negotiated. Larry, of course, has negotiated many financial transactions at times, with difficult bankers or our own directors. Again, he will have applied the basic principles of salesmanship.

"Everyone is quite prepared to be called a negotiator, but few – except professional salesmen – are prepared to admit that every time they negotiate they are involved in selling.

"I shall now prove my case: you and I, Bill, had great difficulty in persuading the Nigerian Government to specify and purchase our range of equipment. They sought three concessions: a larger discount, a change in specification (which we could not meet) and increased spare parts stock, to be held by us in Lagos and purchased by them as required.

"The marketing team had won seventy per cent of the battle. We had got around the discount problem, and the stock-holding demand. But we were up against a most difficult Nigerian engineer who was determined to show his subordinates just how difficult he could be in the pursuit of his requirements. That was when we called you in, Bill, and this is how you tackled the problem: First, you wanted to know everything about Borgannor, the Nigerian engineer. Why was he being so difficult? Had he given us the true reason for the change in the specification? Was he being bribed by competitors? . . . Bill concluded that Borgannor was one of the few incorruptibles there, and he was being difficult because

Charlie Denning, our export salesman, had tended to
ignore him in his determination to get the order, which
had finally to be O.K.'d by Chief Nessar – the one man
who had the authority to place the order. So that was
Rule No. 1, Bill, which you didn't know was pure
salesmanship: *always prepare your case and find out as
much as you can about the buyer and any associates who can
influence the buyer's decision.*

"When we arrived at Lagos, we arranged to meet
Borgannor and I was the only other person present. You
allowed him to talk about himself, about his engineering
expertise, you deferred to his judgement – you went on
like that for two hours. You complimented him on his
technical skills – not flattery, but praise, because he is a
very able person. I was ignored. We had dinner that
evening and still you didn't bring up the technical
problems. What you were doing, Bill, indirectly, was
telling Borgannor that you and he had a lot in common
while intimating that folk like us in the marketing
division couldn't be expected to understand technical
problems.

"Did you know what you were doing, Bill? To use one
of the oldest expressions, now rarely used, you were
selling yourself: but you were not doing it consciously.
You were enjoying talking to a fellow technician. So that
was *Selling Rule No. 2: People prefer to buy from those they
like and who help to build up their importance.*

"Next day, we went to his office. He had his colleagues
with him and I thought now was the time when things
were going to get really difficult. But you handled the
situation superbly, continually stressing the advantages
of keeping to our set specification. You didn't once
disagree with the changes he wanted you to make, but
you kept insisting on the many benefits of keeping to a
standard design. You didn't realise it, Bill, but you were
selling benefits. And that's what selling *is* – building
benefit on benefit in a logical order so that there will

come a time when the benefits outweigh the negatives in the buyer's mind. You were logical in the sequence of your presentation, and you got his agreement step by step – which we, in selling, call *getting 'yes' responses*. So you see, Bill Manley, you are a salesman as much as a production wizard and a negotiator."

Manley said, "Who am I to stop Tom in full flight when he's telling me how brilliant I am?"

Tom smiled and said, "Bill, you and Borgannor got on like a house on fire. You certainly didn't fawn on him – you're not the type – and anyway, those who flatter others rarely reach the negotiating stage, because they are apt to give away all they can give much too early. But you won the day, Bill, and they agreed to accept our standards."

Craig Nelson said, "You have summed up the selling part of negotiating very well, Tom, I hope I can do as well. Shall I take over now and begin with objections?"

"You've mixed up the parts, Craig," said Tom. "We agreed that I would cover objections."

"Sorry," said Nelson with a grin, "it's just that it's a subject I really like dealing with."

"That's being honest at least," said Tom, "you didn't pretend you'd forgotten our arrangement. But I'll be brief, Craig. If objections cannot be answered in a satisfactory manner, the selling function will fail and there will be no subsequent negotiation of any value. Most major objections do arise at the negotiating stage, except for the bombshell types which, I know, will be covered by Craig. As Hugh will know when trying to persuade a trade union official to accept a low pay offer when he is demanding double the amount, most of the objections raised during the early stages are information-seeking objections. For example, *How can you prove that our demand will cause redundancies?* or *We cannot go along with you on guesswork.* These information-seeking objections must be answered satisfactorily, and proof must be given if necessary, so that there can be no last-minute hiccough.

"In professional selling, there are simple techniques used for answering these objections, while major objections, such as price, delivery, change of specification, will usually occur during the negotiating stages. But if a minor objection is brushed aside and not answered satisfactorily, then the negotiations will be difficult, and the outcome in doubt. Never, never ignore an objection – never consider it of little importance, and when the negotiating begins you will start off in a winning position.

"Does that cover the ground, Craig?"

"Yes, right on the nail, Tom."

Angela opened the door. She was accompanied by the general help, carrying a tray of coffee and biscuits. Soon, they were all stretching their legs, and McAllister asked if they might make some 'phone calls.

After the break Tom asked to be allowed to say a final few words. Naturally, there were no objections.

He said, "I'd like to summarise: selling precedes negotiating – and negotiation can only succeed if four conditions are satisfied:

1 The buyer – that is the person who has to buy the idea, must have complete confidence in the integrity of the negotiator.

2 The buyer must know that the offer made will meet his need.

3 The buyer is aware of all the benefits to be derived from the offer.

4 The buyer has agreed, step by step, with the negotiator during the preliminary selling, and feels that all his minor objections have been answered satisfactorily.

"And now, at last, it's over to you, Craig."

Nelson rose slowly to his feet. "If you don't mind me

standing up," he said, "I think better on my feet."

He paused, then continued, "Tom has correctly summed up negotiating as being the giving or taking of concessions. If the build-up is right, the way to closing the deal, or shaking hands on a decision, is clear cut. The buyer is convinced and is prepared to buy, or accept an offer, or maybe settle a strike. But he will not do this without a concession or concessions – possibly a higher discount, longer credit, a change in specification, additional holidays with pay . . . The negotiator might be prepared to agree to a slightly higher discount if he, in his turn, can receive a concession to make up for it – for example, if he can get cash on the nail. To achieve concessions, buyers use different techniques. They can be brutal, or all sweet sunshine. They can plead, almost with tears in their eyes, or snort like a bull to show their annoyance. They will lie (or, at least, stretch points) or be completely honest . . . but will not budge an inch. The buyer wants to win – but so does the negotiator. First you must know your own position. Are you negotiating from strength or weakness? If you have a monopoly you don't have to negotiate; you demand, so long as you are aware of the fact that there is always a future, and if you don't think of the future, that demand could catch up with you some time. When the Saudis put up oil prices in 1973 there was no negotiating whatsoever – they weren't going to give any concessions, they were in a winning situation. But things have changed a little since then. If you are up against a buyer who need not give a single concession, you take his crumbs – there is no alternative. No ploys will work under these conditions, but as in the case of the oil situation, this state of affairs does not last for ever. There will come a time when a buyer must buy and a seller sell on equal terms; when both want a deal closed. That, in fact, happens most of the time; house buyers negotiate with house sellers, and production directors negotiate with works councils.

There is give and take, but one side nearly always wins. Tom's story about his negotiations in Nigeria emphasises a most important factor – *know your buyer*.

"Here are the four most difficult types of buyer that we all come up against at times. Let's think about them, and start with *Second-hand Joe*.

"*Second-hand Joe* is not really tough, but his managing director or union secretary – or even his wife – is tough, and Joe has been told in no uncertain manner that he must get A or B or C – which could be a discount, a contract for not less than five years with his company, or shorter working hours. But *Second-hand Joe* pretends to be tough because he is scared to give way.

"The only way to tackle Joe is to bring in your own back stage gorilla to make it clear that you have been given the parameters of your offer, that these have now been reached and that there can be no addition or the gorilla will be after your blood – and you don't like bleeding! Make sure that *Second-hand Joe* gets the message, which he can pass on when the deal is closed – and Joe usually has the authority to close the deal. He is only scared that he will be told he should have done better. There must be no equivocation; be honest, give all possible concessions and then be rocklike in your determination that there is no more to give. You will win more often than you will lose if you take this attitude.

"The opposite to Joe is *I-wish-I-could George*. George is very friendly, with an arm around the shoulder approach, but his objective is to wheedle major concessions by telling you that the final say is with, for example, his managing director.

"There isn't a word of truth in this 'I-wish-I-could' attitude. He has been given the right to make decisions, but unlike Joe, who is scared of the man above and frightened of making a mistake, George uses the man upstairs as a reason for pulling out your finger nails, if this is what he is after.

"Don't be fooled by George! He is tough, and not a friend. You deal with him, if you reach an impasse, by suggesting that your managing director will telephone his managing director, and explain how he – George – has done his best and you, the negotiator, have done your best, but it was obvious that a top level meeting was necessary in the interests of both sides. The ploy usually works. George, if he feels he has a reasonable result, will capitulate. He knows his bluff has been called.

"The third is *I'm Always Right Jack*. Jack is, possibly, the most difficult of all to handle. He can be a technician, or a store buyer who believes he knows what is best for his customers, or a union official who is always ready to call a strike and fight whoever is in power. Yes, Jack's rather a difficult man, and the only way I have ever got the better of him is to allow him to find faults in me. Let him pinpoint my mistakes – and I make deliberate mistakes about some fact or some issue, which he always jumps on. I can then apologise and admit that I was wrong, and more often than not this modifies Jack's stance and he will then bend a little in his attitude. He may even give way on a concession.

"Finally, we have *First-past-the-post Peter*. Peter always has to win. He could be a first-class golfer – he wants to win so badly that he would not even concede a two-inch putt. No one, he boasts, ever gets the better of him!

"There is only one way to tackle Peter: keep the one concession which you know he will want, and which you might grant, in the background, but argue, and argue, and argue again on every minor concession – every minor change he wants. Argue as if your life depended on the results, but eventually, let him win each concession. Then, when the crisis point arrives – a difficult change in specification, or a bigger discount – you stand firm and mean it. With so many victories under his belt Peter, surprisingly, often gives way on the one which really matters.

"Well, these are the four problem buyers. Most of the rest don't fall into categories; they are typical of all mankind – some short-tempered, some most equable, some talkers, some listeners, but most are reasonable people, trying to do their best for country, company, union, and with them all the standard techniques work at some time or another.

Nelson glanced at his watch before continuing. It showed twelve noon. "I have a surprise for you after lunch," he went on. Lunch had been scheduled for twelve-thirty. "At two o'clock a friend of mine will be arriving – Sam Roskoff – you'll like him! We have given our negotiating act right across the USA."

McAllister had known what was happening, but the four directors were puzzled and anxious to hear more.

Larry Duckworth broke the silence, saying, "You're a surprising character, Craig. You have twice created great wealth, so you obviously don't need the fees. Why do you do these negotiating sessions? I wouldn't if I were in your place."

Craig Nelson stroked his chin, looked thoughtful for a moment, then said, "The answer lies, probably, in the difference between the British and the Yanks. We never believe anything is going to last for ever, unless we make it do so. We never sit back on our laurels. Our axiom is that either you keep going or you get out. Sam is a vice-president of my organisation; one day he will take over from me, but we're in a tricky business. Stars are fickle, and authors are just as unpredictable. After all, I took most of my business away from All-Star Associates – they're right down the drain now, and every new agency is out gunning for me. We are only as good as our negotiating ability. So we go around the country to universities and management centres to keep our name as top negotiators right in the forefront. All our fees are given to local charities. Is that answer acceptable?"

They all voiced or nodded their agreement, although

Larry could not imagine himself doing one night stands as a preventive measure.

"And what are you and Mr Roskoff going to do?" asked Tom.

"May we leave that until he arrives?" answered Nelson.

"Of course!"

"There are a couple more points I'd like to make before we have our break. The first is to forget the old tag that the ideal outcome of a negotiation is a fifty-fifty draw, with both sides equally satisfied. The objective of a negotiator is to win – and that is also the objective of the buyer. And by winning I mean at least sixty-forty in favour of the negotiator. This applies to all negotiating. It doesn't apply, however, when you are negotiating within your own business – for example, when engaging new staff or arranging a contract for an executive. Then, the terms should be on a fifty-fifty basis.

"The only other exception is when a salesman is selling goods, or products, or services to a buyer. The power, then, is nearly always with the buyer, because the buyer has a choice. There are always competitors waiting to pounce. The salesman, therefore, has to be a really tough negotiator if he is to achieve a fifty-fifty result. If, then, he manages sixty-forty, it usually means that the buyer needs him a little more than he needs the buyer. But the salesman must never be the loser; the result can be fifty-fifty, but he must always fight for a higher percentage in his favour.

"Summed up, then, negotiating is the art of give and take – and the one who wins gives least and takes most. Too many negotiators are not tough enough. Let me make it clear, I agree with being gentle, provided that by that we mean respect for the other person. No one can criticise your Maggie Thatcher for her manners, but when she negotiates, she negotiates to win.

"Toughness doesn't mean being inflexible. Maggie

Thatcher quickly switched her stance over Zimbabwe (then Rhodesia) when she realised that toughness was getting her nowhere. So what we are after is tough flexibility!

"Now Sam and I shall be concentrating on the final stages of negotiations. I want to consider for a moment – there is still time before lunch – pre-negotiating strategy; and remember, first we must look at our own qualifications now and again, to make sure that we know what to look for in our managers who also have to negotiate. Before negotiating begins we have to think of these points: One, ask yourself what will the buyer's demands be, both in standard concessions and extra concessions? Identify those factors.

"Two, the more you can learn about his background, plans, the strengths and weaknesses of his organisation, the better placed you will be to win.

"Three, now do something unusual: Write down all the questions you would ask of yourself were you the other person, including questions about the weaknesses of your offer.

"Four, determine the maximum concessions you are able to offer, and then be equally determined to give as little as possible. Know, and appreciate, the cost of each concession you give. You can only be flexible within set parameters.

"Five, remember the buyer always exaggerates. When the union leader says that the boys are all behind him, he means, possibly fifty per cent. When a subordinate tells you he has had half a dozen offers, he means one – and that one not for sure! When the buyer says he can get ten per cent discount, he means five per cent. Plan to overcome these exaggerations by facts you can produce.

"Six, plan in advance when you want to introduce a concession. This may be preferable to waiting for the buyer's request. If you pre-empt the issue it will often lessen the strength of the buyer's demands.

"Seven, decide what concessions *you* will demand. These come under the headings of *essential, reasonable,* and *hopeful*. There can be no compromise with the essential and that must be made clear to the buyer. What you consider to be reasonable could be the subject of give and take, but again, you must know how far you are prepared to go to enforce the reasonable. The hopeful can often be used as a bartering weapon – an apparent climbing down or giving way.

"Eight, many buyers consider it a challenge to their authority if they are quoted a firm, unnegotiable price. They like to feel that they have influenced a price concession. Give yourself room to manoeuvre.

"Nine, don't think negatively before the meeting begins. If you keep reminding yourself that you are willing to take less, almost invariably you will take less.

"Ten, decide in advance what help you will require – possibly the assistance of an accountant, an engineer, a service manager, a designer . . . It is bad negotiating to ask for an adjournment to enable you to seek such advice.

"Eleven, always be ready to make a buyer work hard for a concession.

"Twelve, check your qualifications as a negotiator.

"Let's take a look at ourselves and ask some pertinent questions:

"Do we force ourselves to be patient?

"Do we plan meticulously for every eventuality?

"Do we think clearly enough to handle the unexpected, which invariably occurs during negotiations?

"Do we have the ability to define the real issue quickly? Buyers always introduce side issues to detract from the importance of the real one.

"Do we have the ability to handle conflicts?

"Do we know when, and when not, to take risks? How far we can bluff?

"Do we listen intently, all the time? The emphasis is on *all of the time*. Nothing is irrelevant. Because you have

heard similar statements, stories, questions, objections
. . . before, there is no reason why you should not listen
just as intently to them again – otherwise you might miss
an important issue."

Nelson had been talking very rapidly. He hardly
seemed to pause for breath, but he stopped now to take a
deep breath before continuing: "One final point to
remember when trading concessions: we have to justify
each one that we give away, and also to justify each one
we ask for. Although you are going for a sixty-forty per
cent victory, try to leave the buyer believing that he has
had the best of the deal, and if negotiating fails, leave the
buyer open for further discussion."

The timing was perfect. Angela arrived to announce
not only that luncheon was ready, but also that Mr Sam
Roskoff had arrived with apologies for being early, and
Angela immediately insisted that Sam must join them for
luncheon.

The four directors had all expected Sam Roskoff to be
a fat, cigar-smoking New Yorker. They were wrong. He
was tall, thin, balding, with an aesthetic appearance.

Lunch was a hilarious affair. Angela had provided the
ideal meal. Her table was laden with every type of dainty
snack, which could be washed down with Chablis – a
help-yourself meal. They could take their pick of chicken
legs, cocktail sausages, smoked salmon on brown bread,
home-made pâté on toast, and other delicacies.

Sam told anecdote after anecdote, all related to the film
world. He concluded with a story of his first meeting
with the legendary Sam Goldwyn. He thought it a proper
story for the negotiating session that was to follow.

Roskoff said, "I was younger and brasher – also, I was
big-headed and looking forward to the confrontation. I
was ushered into the great man's office by a delectable
blonde. He looked affable enough, and greeted me
warmly, as though he had known me for years. At that
time I was agent for Lois Tallent – I thought up the name

for her, by the way. I considered it very good at the time – now, I think it's terrible! But we all believed she was set to go places, so I told Sam Goldwyn what I wanted and he listened carefully. After a short period of skirmishing I said firmly, "I'm only asking for two thousand dollars a week."

"Goldwyn's face changed from kindness to ferocity and he replied, 'You're not asking for two thousand dollars a week, you're asking for fifteen hundred dollars – and I'm giving the lady a thousand!' And with that he stood up and showed me to the door."

Sam Roskoff concluded, "On that day I learned an important lesson about negotiating – *never be misled by a friendly appearance.*"

The afternoon session was opened by Craig Nelson. The room had been rearranged to enable a role-playing scene to be enacted. In front of the french windows stood a table, between two chairs. The four directors and Don McAllister sat facing the role players, Sam and Craig, who were seated at the table, sideways on to their audience.

Craig Nelson turned towards the directors and began, "We're now going to demonstrate some negotiating gimmicks plus techniques, all of which will, I hope, bring out a lesson. These lessons won't be new to you, but as I have been told, the idea of this meeting is to get back to fundamentals. Sam and I will be playing negotiator and buyer – switching roles now and again. In this scene, we have reached the stage when we both want a settlement. All minor objections have been overcome, and thus our final meeting may have been preceded by days or weeks of discussion.

"The negotiating stage is now starting, with both sides seeking concessions and each of us wanting to give away as little as possible. We shall begin with a typical situation. The furniture in my house has been partly destroyed or damaged by fire and flood. The insurance assessor has called to make an offer. I am the buyer, and I want to negotiate as good a settlement as possible, while Sam, acting on behalf of the insurance company, wants to make a settlement that will satisfy his management."

****

Nelson then turned away from his audience and said, "It's difficult for me, Mr Roskoff, to understand the ways of insurance companies. I have made a fair claim for seventeen thousand, five hundred dollars, and you offer me fifteen thousand. Why?"

"Because, as I have told you, that, in our opinion, is what the furniture is now worth."

"Why should I accept your opinion?"

"There's more to it than that."

"I'm sure there is! Please tell me how you arrive at your figure."

"What?"

"Tell me how you arrive at the figure of fifteen thousand dollars."

"We take into consideration the age of the furniture; remember, you couldn't produce any initial receipts."

"But suppose the furniture has improved with age – long waxing and polishing can bring out the best in wood, just as special creams can feed leathers. How do you arrive at the difference, in view of the fact that you have never previously inspected the furniture?"

"We work on averages."

"How, then, have you arrived at your average?"

Nelson stopped, and stood up. Turning to his audience he said, "We need not go on, but the ploy used is in the phrase: How do you arrive at . . . ? When negotiating concessions there can often be no exact justification for an offer or a demand, and by continually using that one sentence you can put things in true perspective, whether you are the buyer or the negotiator. Once you have pinpointed the fact that guesswork has been involved you are well on your way to winning. O.K.?"

Everyone nodded.

"Now," went on Nelson, "we are going to try something different. We are going to negotiate the sale of machinery – any kind of machinery – but involving an outlay of a million dollars. We have been negotiating for weeks, and have decided that the day of decision has arrived. This time I shall be the technical director responsible for placing the order, and Sam is the sales director of the company manufacturing the machinery. I shall begin."

****

He turned away from the audience: "Mr Roskoff, we are getting nowhere fast. You won't budge on price or agree with our need for increased speed of the robot pickup. You must admit that I have given way on delivery, initial stage payments, and lubrication channels. But I am not prepared to give way any more."

"Mr Nelson, if I called you a tough negotiator you would get even tougher. If I said you were a skilled negotiator your skills would then beat me into the ground. But I'll take that risk. You are as tough as anyone I have ever met, and no one can ever have any doubt about your negotiating skills. I can't be as tough because you are the buyer, I can't be as skilful because my skill won't motivate you to buy; but I can present you with facts, and although you are tough and skilful, I know you will not dispute facts. You agreed to an extension of three months on the delivery date, Mr Nelson, but be honest, the roadworks necessary to tie in with the installation won't be completed until then. You agreed to a twenty per cent first stage payment instead of fifteen per cent, but, Mr Nelson, your company has more liquid resources than many a country."

"Hey, hey – wait a minute," interrupted Nelson. "Maybe you're right, maybe not, but if I were so tough I wouldn't have given a penny more or agreed to one day later on delivery."

"That, Mr Nelson, is because you're tough, but fair. As far as the lubricating channels are concerned, I told you we could change them for you, but that would have to be covered by increased costs. Now let me put this point to you; by paring and rethinking I got the price down to within three per cent of the competitor's offer you told me about. That was one helluva concession, in view of our quality, which is the best in the world. Frankly, I didn't think it was possible, and I don't think you did, either. Now, can't we compromise? You agree with our standard robot pickup which, I assure you – no, promise you – will give you all the speed you require, and I'll go to the extra cost of making the changes in the lubricating channels."

Sam stopped talking, stood up, and faced the directors.

"What lessons are we emphasising here?" he asked.

Hugh Fairley said, "You very cleverly introduced justifiable praise because, undoubtedly, Craig is meant to be a tough, skilled negotiator, and while flattery can kill negotiating, justifiable praise can soften the most stubborn of buyers."

Lawson said, "I think the most important point you made was in minimising the concessions that Craig, the buyer, had made. You almost wrote them off as perfectly meaningless, which is always a good negotiating ploy."

Manley commented, "You're using a dodge that I've used over and over again. You were trading concessions, but you won the important point – you won on price – you weren't going to match the competitor's offer."

Duckworth remained silent, so Nelson said to Sam, "I

think we're wasting our time – they know it all!"

Good natured laughter was followed by Lawson's comment, "I am enjoying your act tremendously, and your reminders to us of what negotiating is really about. I'm looking forward to what's coming next!"

Nelson said, "Our next scenario will show up common negotiating mistakes. This time I am going to try and negotiate a million dollar loan from Sam, who is a bank official. Now I'll begin:

★★★★★★★★★★

"You will agree, Mr Roskoff, that our company has a second to none reputation. It would be completely unfair for you to insist on personal guarantees. Also your interest rate is too high. I can get a better deal at the Colony Bank."

"Mr Nelson, if you could get better rates elsewhere you would not be here."

"That is an insulting remark!"

"It was not meant to be. You made a statement, and I reacted to that statement."

"I'm here because you have been our bankers for fifteen years."

"I appreciate that, Mr Nelson, but you must understand that I have the bank's interest to consider first."

"Are you telling me," Nelson somehow became red in the face, "that you place nothing on loyalty, friendly co-operation – call it anything you like? Are you telling me that a good relationship means nothing to your lousy bank?"

"Please, please, Mr Nelson – let us discuss matters in a rational manner."

"I'm going." Nelson stood up.

"As you wish." Sam shrugged his shoulders.

Nelson didn't move, then hesitantly he sat down again. "O.K.," he said, "well, if you'll forget the personal guarantees we'll agree to pay the additional one per cent – not two per cent, mind. That, I think, is fair compromise."

"I can't do that. Both you and Mr Reynolds, a major shareholder in your business and a director, should accept the responsibility and be prepared to guarantee the debt."

"Why?"

"Because you and he are the company in our eyes, and it is to you and him that we must look for payment if there should be a default."

"You have the shares."

Roskoff said, "But they are only of value if your expansion plans succeed and your profitability increases."

"You have the deeds of our property."

"They are already sixty per cent mortgaged. Ours would have to be a second mortgage."

"Look, I'll have to talk to Harry Reynolds. May I use your telephone?"

"Certainly, use that one" – Roskoff conveyed the impression of pushing an imaginary telephone across the table. "I'll be back in five minutes."

Nelson turned to the audience and counted – "One, two, three, four, five. Five minutes gone – we're back together again."

Nelson continued, "O.K., Harry agrees – but not our wives."

"I'm afraid that's not good enough," said Roskoff.

"You're drawing blood!"

"I'm only doing my job."

Nelson sighed. "O.K. Can I use the telephone again?"

The previous procedure was repeated, including the count-off of the minutes.

Nelson said, "Let me get this straight: You want all four of us to guarantee the million dollars. Does that guarantee hold until the loan is repaid in full?"

"Yes."

"But what about the property? You have a forty per cent safeguard there."

"Very well, then, we'll reduce your guarantee to seventy-five per cent of the loan, and we'll take a second mortgage."

"And you'll agree to lower the interest rate by one per cent, O.K.?"

"No."

"They ought to promote you to chief money-lender!" said Nelson.

Roskoff ignored the sarcasm and said, "You're asking for a substantial sum. I'm willing to reassess the interest rate, but that means checking with head office."

"And that means another delay!" cried Nelson. "It's damnable!"

"And that's enough," said Roskoff, as they both stood up.

Once again, the audience applauded.

Nelson said, "This, of course, is all fundamentals for you, but it isn't for the managers who attend our seminars. And never mislead yourselves into believing that we in the USA are better negotiators than the British. We're not! In fact, from the point of view of diplomacy, you're way ahead of us. We have made seven cardinal negotiating errors – I'm sure you have spotted them all, Hugh." He had wisely chosen Hugh Fairley because he knew Fairley, as personnel director, was responsible for all courses including those on negotiating.

Fairley said, "I wouldn't guarantee I'll get them all right, but here goes: One, the negotiator must always strive to save the face of the buyer, and never bluff unless there is a certainty that the bluff will work. Craig intimated that all bankers were queueing up to give him a loan. This was a threat. If the manager had given way under duress he would have lost face, so the bluff didn't work. If Craig could have gone elsewhere he shouldn't have said a word about it but should first have gone elsewhere, to see if he could get better terms.

"The second point in negotiating is that it is often of little use appealing to long-term friendly relationships as a reason for the buyer to give way. Craig used the fifteen year association appeal, and later, the loyalty appeal. This rarely works and it is often embarrassing.

"Three, Craig, you lost your temper with Sam. A good negotiator may pretend to lose his temper if he believes it will have an effect, but that is what I call a controlled loss of temper, used for a purpose. To lose one's temper regardless of consequences can have a disastrous effect on negotiations.

"Four, Craig pretended he was about to leave. He stood up and it was tantamount to ending the interview. But once more, this was bluff, and it didn't work.

"Five, it was wrong to telephone the co-director, Harry Reynolds, and later the wives. Before negotiations commence the parameters should have been decided upon by all concerned. Craig should have known whether or not Harry or the wives would agree to being guarantors.

"Six, Craig was being sarcastic to the banker when he likened him to a money-lender. The banker did the right thing by ignoring the sarcastic remark. Sarcasm can never be a winning ploy in negotiating. It is always a loser.

"Seven, the bank manager didn't have to clear with head office. It was Sam Roskoff's turn to bluff. At that time, Nelson should have made a firm offer and tried to settle on the spot."

"One hundred per cent right," said Nelson.

Larry Duckworth said, "I missed the sarcastic remark."

Bill Manley added, "And I overlooked the weakness of telephoning for guidance."

Roskoff said, "Never, during negotiation, should a negotiator have to telephone some superior for advice. He should be in a position to make all the decisions, unless it has been made clear from the beginning that he cannot conclude the negotiations without referring back."

Everyone was thoroughly enjoying the role playing, and Manley said "What's the next one about?"

"Negotiating book rights," said Nelson.

"That sounds useful," said Lawson. "I've set my mind on writing a book about all the goings-on at Huntley's one day."

"You wouldn't do that!" said Manley. "We'd all sue you for libel."

Nelson interrupted the badinage with, "I'm now the publisher's managing director, and Sam will be what he is – the agent – selling an author's work for as much as he can get."

★★★★★★★★★★

Sam and Craig once more sat down at the table, and Sam said, "I can only repeat, this is a block-buster – and you know it! It's Derek Sullivan's best ever. It will sell over a million copies in hardback alone, and I can't settle for less than two hundred thousand dollars advance."

Nelson answered, "In the present state of the market even well-known authors no longer sell in millions. I repeat, the best I can do is one hundred thousand dollars – you can take it or leave it!"

"If that's your attitude I'll have to consider whether or not I can offer you Sara Tulloch's new romance."

Nelson said, "Let's deal with one thing at a time. There is no way I can consider an advance of two hundred thousand dollars – unless of course you also give us the paperback rights."

"Impossible! It must go to tender. You'll have the

same opportunity as others of making an offer."

"How about the film rights, then? I had David Simmonds the producer on the telephone yesterday. He's heard about the latest Sullivan and he's very keen on the film rights."

"I know David well," said Sam.

"Of course you do!" answered Nelson. "But he happens to be my wife's cousin, and they're real buddies. And you know what film producers' promises are worth! Even you couldn't get Sullivan's last book filmed. Let's not bicker," Nelson went on. "I'll call our film rights negotiator Leslie Barstow. He's read the book, and he knows the percentage as far as the film is concerned."

They pretended that Barstow had been sent for, and there was a discussion. Nelson turned to the audience, explaining that Barstow had emphasised the difficulties of getting any book filmed, but conceded that the opportunity to tie up with David Simmonds was too good to miss.

Sam said, "Let's settle the deal. Make the advance a hundred and seventy-five thousand dollars – and that's my final offer. And you can negotiate with David for the film rights – but if David won't take it, the film rights revert to us. How about that?"

"There's nothing certain," said Nelson, "and if David does say no – and that, of course, is always possible, in spite of our close association – I'm still left with giving away a hundred and seventy-five thousand dollars, an advance which is more than my board have decided is reasonable."

Roskoff thought for a moment, then said, "Look, let's telephone Lionel Parsons. He's the president of your association and he's a friend of both of us. He's also friendly with Sullivan, and knows his books well. We can ask him what he considers to be a fair advance."

"No," said Nelson, "that's quite out of the question."

"We're deadlocked then," said Sam, "so let's call it all

off now and we can both think about it."

Sam stood up and, turning to the audience, said, "Now you have to attune your minds to the fact that two weeks have elapsed.

"During those two weeks I would have been considering every alternative. Could I get a better deal elsewhere? Possibly! But there is no better publisher than Nelson's firm, who could guarantee that the book would be exploited to the full. I would consider whether there was any different strategy I could adopt. Should I be nicer, or should I be tougher? I would have been consulting associates to see if they had any ideas which could bridge the gap.

"I had to consider the risk. If I gave way and accepted a much lower advance Sullivan might then decide to change his agent. Finally, I had to consider: was Nelson bluffing, or did he really want the book at all costs? It was certain that behind the scenes his marketing director would be pressing him to buy.

"I decided that the chances were that Nelson was bluffing."

Roskoff then said, "Remembering all that, we are now back in Nelson's office."

They sat down and Nelson, turning to Sam, said, "I have discussed the matter with the full board, and we are prepared to go to a hundred and twenty-five thousand dollars advance, plus the first shot at the film rights, with David."

"No."

"I'm sorry, then," said Nelson, "you have obviously lost sight of present day conditions in the book trade – and Sullivan didn't do so well with his last book."

"He still headed the best seller list for three months. I've spoken to Derek Sullivan and he was mad with me for even considering anything less than two hundred thousand. He now insists on a quarter of a million advance."

Nelson said, "He must think we're here solely to risk our money on his behalf. We are not. We can't afford a gamble. We are here to make a profit, and we don't make a profit until the books are sold and paid for. But we can't continue like this. Let's see if we can arrange a compromise. How about Derek Sullivan giving us the first rights on his next two books, instead of the usual one? We'll have the first film rights to sell to David Simmonds, but if he fails us, the rights will revert to you. You will also show us Sara Tulloch's new romantic novel, before you show it to any other publisher, and we'll have the first rights to publish it."

"And if I agree?"

"We'll make the advance a hundred and fifty thousand dollars."

Sam turned to the audience and said, "He was bluffing – they do want the book. I've won!" Then he turned back to Nelson and said, "Not quite enough – but I'll shake hands now on a hundred and seventy thousand dollars advance. It means I have come down by thirty thousand dollars on my original request and eighty thousand on Derek's demands. He'll probably kill me, but I'll take that chance. How about it?"

Nelson stood up and the two men shook hands.

Lawson said, "When I write my book, will you be my agent, Sam?"

"Sure! I'll sign you up right now."

There was more good humoured banter, then Sam Roskoff said, "I'm sure you all got all the lessons from that act. You can each take it in turn to answer, that's what I usually do at seminars. You've heard it all before, Don, so you can start off."

McAllister said, "Craig Nelson shouldn't have tried bluff so early, when he said take it or leave it, and then immediately capitulated by continuing the negotiations. By that action alone Sam knew he could strike a better bargain."

"Good! It's your turn, Larry."

"I'm not very well up in these affairs," said Duckworth, "but it seemed to me that Craig Nelson won a point when he got the film rights. It meant he could play around with these rights for quite a while, even if his wife's cousin didn't buy. It was unlikely that Sam Roskoff would kill the deal on principle if he came up with a reasonable offer from someone else."

"That's right. Craig did win a point there."

"And he won another point," said Lawson, "when he sent for his film rights executive. It's always a good thing to send for an expert to emphasise a factor during negotiations, provided that expert is nearby."

"Exactly!" said Sam. "And what are your thoughts, Bill?"

"I suppose Sam won," said Bill, "when he suggested calling the director of the trade association, and Nelson refused to do so. He refused because he knew that the director's advice might possibly be to find the true market by going to other publishers. And Nelson clearly didn't want that to happen – definitely a point to the agent." Manley continued, "Then Sam, knowing that they had reached deadlock, called for a break in negotiations. I've done that many times – especially when I have known that I was well on the way to winning, but I needed some extra help before I could get my concession."

Hugh Fairley said, "Sam increased his demand to a quarter of a million dollars. Whether that was true or false didn't matter – he could have been bluffing, but he need not have been. But he knew that during the two weeks there would have been pressure on Nelson, and he felt he could afford a bluff which might worry Nelson. When Nelson suggested a compromise, Sam knew he had won. But at the same time Sam had let Nelson think he had won as well, by upping the demand. Nelson could then report to his board that he had saved them eighty thousand dollars. So it was a good all round conclusion."

There was some discussion, and they all agreed that the day's work had been both enjoyable and informative. When they were about to wind up the meeting Nelson said, "One final point: Always remember when negotiating to think of an alternative if you are the loser. We can't win all the time, but an alternative can often keep the options open."

Everyone thanked Sam and Craig profusely.

Later, McAllister said, "Now for our next two meetings we are due to cover time management and delegating. It doesn't matter in which order."

"May I have a word?" said Fairley.

"Sure, carry on," said Don.

"There's one aspect of communication in leadership that we haven't put in our agenda. All managers have to speak in public at some time or another – especially the directors – and some of them are not too good at it. We are holding a three-day public speaking course at our training centre. I know it's a lot to ask, but don't you think it would be a good plan if we could all attend? It would also do our image a world of good – I'm talking about the image of our training centre. When it gets around that the top brass have attended, management will be queueing up – the very thing I want to happen, because in the past the course has been poorly attended; the managers keep making excuses when I know the real problem is their fear of looking foolish in front of other managers. We've got to get them along, and this is a wonderful opportunity if you will all agree and I'm sure it will do us all good!"

No one was very keen on the idea, but Hugh's

persuasive personality prevailed, and finally, all four directors promised to attend the next public speaking course.

11   Some Straight Talking

The usual monthly meeting to consider the management accounts, held in the boardroom at Huntley House, commenced at eight-thirty am and finished at four-thirty pm, with no time wasted. Huntley himself made sure that the minds of his directors were concentrated on the most important factors only. The directors were mainly concerned with cash flow, cash forecasts, stock levels, length of outstanding accounts, overall costs, and contribution percentages. No irrelevancies were ever introduced at meetings under Huntley's chairmanship.

After the chief executive had left, the directors remained behind to check with regional directors on account discrepancies. On such days all regional executives stayed by their telephones. By six o'clock each task had been completed.

Manley said, "I've been thinking about our attending the public speaking course. Do you consider it wise for top brass to suddenly descend on managers already nervous about taking tests to prove their ability as good verbal communicators?"

Fairley said, "I thought someone would be objecting after the initial enthusiasm had worn off. What makes you think, Bill, that you will fare any better than anyone else?"

"That's not the point. Do we have to prove ourselves in front of others?"

Lawson asked, "You don't think the managers will

freeze up if we are there? They're bound to be scared, as Bill said."

Hugh interrupted, "Tim Currie has assured me that there will be no fear of that. No one will be made to look foolish. At the end of the course he insists they will all be eager to demonstrate their speaking skills."

Duckworth said, "I'm not altogether in favour, but we can't back down now. Remember when the meetings as a whole were suggested by Don we weren't too keen, but we've all agreed that they have succeeded in their objective."

Manley said, "O.K., I'll go along with it – but I've got a lot on my plate at the moment."

Duckworth said, "I'd like to raise another matter – one that is giving us all concern. Roland is about to retire. He's going to hand over the keys of the office, but to whom? If we assume – and knowing Roland it is only an assumption, because he's a master at doing the un-expected – that he won't look outside for his replace-ment, it must be one of us four. I can't believe that he needs another six months or a year to evaluate us. There isn't anything new for him to learn, and therefore I am of the opinion – and I stressed this earlier – that he is waiting for McAllister's report. In spite of what Don said, I believe that he is going to form judgements on us."

"And what if that is right?" said Lawson. "It won't alter anything. None of us is going to act differently in order to impress Don McAllister. We'll just have to let it ride."

Duckworth said, "Shouldn't we be open with each other now so that we know each other's views? So far as I'm concerned, if the position went to Tom or Bill I should look elsewhere for a chief executive post. Would the same apply to Tom or Bill if I should receive the marshal's baton? Shouldn't we now, for the sake of our future – and the future of the company – express our

views honestly? First, can I have a vote? Shall I proceed
with my argument or would you prefer that each of us
considers his own future, irrespective of how that
decision affects others?"

Manley said, "I appreciate that you don't want to work
under me or Tom. Fair enough! But you're placing us in
a most difficult position. If we vote we may be commit-
ting ourselves to a policy which may go against our
judgements in six months' time. But not voting for
further discussion is tantamount to implying that we each
want to think only of ourselves and to hell with everyone
else!"

"That's not right," said Duckworth. "If we vote for a
discussion we need not commit ourselves, but we can, at
least, prepare for the future. For the past months we
have all considered every factor, and have turned over in
our minds a hundred times what our reaction will be to
Roland's decision. We do, therefore, each of us have a
fair idea of what action we'll take. I'm prepared to state
my case, and you can follow if you wish."

Duckworth was showing his strength, and no one
wished to appear weak in comparison. Taking the silence
as assent Duckworth said, "None of us is indispensable.
If we were all killed in a plane crash tomorrow, within six
months Roland would have another first-class team
around him. Don't let's mislead ourselves on that score.
But I believe that I'm just a little bit more indispensable
than others because of my overall knowledge of the
financial affairs of Huntley's. It might take longer to
replace me, but that's all. However, in to-day's economic
climate there is a shortage of successful financial directors
with experience of large company activities. I have been
head-hunted three times, and each offer was for financial
director and managing director designate. Therefore, I
should have no fear of leaving Huntley's if he took any
action with which I disagreed. Now what would make me
disagree with Roland's decision? I can't work under you,

Bill, much as I respect your ability as production director. We've disagreed too often over factory and machinery investments. I have a high regard for you, Bill – but I couldn't work under you.

"The same applies to you, Tom. You're one of the best marketing men in the country – no doubt about that! But you're also a big spender, and I believe you might be inclined to take undue risks if you were the chief executive.

"I'd be quite happy to work under you, Hugh; I respect your all-round ability, your great understanding of people, and your general all-round knowledge, which is a must for a chief executive. Also, I believe you have the vision to expand the organisation.

"That, gentlemen, is a summing up of my future involvement with the company."

There followed a few seconds of uncomfortable silence, then Hugh Fairley said simply, "Thank you, Larry. We all appreciate your honesty."

Tom was the most upset. "For some reason," he said, "I have the name for being an indiscriminate spender of the company's money. Larry, you know that isn't true. I am prepared to defend the accusation in front of Roland Huntley, when I shall demand exact details of my so-called rash expenditure."

Just bluffing, thought Duckworth.

Lawson continued, "I think I could make a very good chief executive – and I could also work very well under you, Larry."

"Thank you," said Duckworth, not attempting to enlarge on his views.

Bill Manley said, "I believe I'm the right person to be the next chairman and managing director. While marketing is of great importance, if we don't produce the right goods at the right prices, they can't be sold. I've also proved that I can get the best out of a work force. My weakness, as Larry knows, is the financial field. That is why I have not always been able to win my argument for increased expenditure on machinery or new plant. But if you leave because of me, Larry, I could find a man with your capabilities within three months."

And that's put you down, Larry, thought Manley – and they could all read his mind.

He continued in a more conciliatory manner, "But Larry, don't misunderstand me. I should prefer to work under you if you were given the post. I could also work under Hugh. I couldn't work happily under you, Tom; we've had too many disagreements in the past. You have also always sided with sales against production – but if you get the job, Tom, I'll still give you my best."

"Thank you, Bill," said Tom Lawson.

Lawson knew there was no possibility of his resigning for any reason; he had too little capital to see him through a crisis. Also, he was very highly paid and there were few firms that could match the total package generously provided by Roland Huntley.

He continued, "I believe that we live in a world of over-production, and therefore only a company with dynamic marketing can survive. I'd be a damned good chief executive, but if I don't get the job, as I said, I'll work happily under you, Hugh, you, Bill, or you, Larry."

Hugh Fairley said, "Larry, you've done us a service by bringing our thoughts out into the open. We know now how we stand. I shall give of my best, whoever I serve under – but naturally, I am hoping to be appointed by Roland as the next chief executive."

Manley said, "Let's approach Roland, and ask for a decision."

They all disagreed with the suggestion. Roland would retire in his own good time, he would not be pushed into an early decision – such a request could result in his staying on.

"How about discussing it with Don McAllister?" suggested Tom Lawson.

Again, the others disagreed, explaining that when they had earlier had a discussion with Don, he had semi-denied that he could influence Roland Huntley in any way.

On their way home, they thought again about their discussion on the future. Larry was happy. He could now tell Huntley honestly that the other three directors would certainly work under him. No one would leave if he were appointed. Tom Lawson was the most concerned, until he thought of a brilliant idea, namely to suggest to Huntley that no one person could ever replace him as chief executive. Why not, for the good of the company, appoint joint managing directors – him, because of his marketing expertise, and Larry for his financial knowledge? That should appeal to Roland, because then he would know that Larry would be in a position to argue against what he might consider to be unnecessary expenditure. He would suggest to Roland that he would even agree to Larry having the final say over all expenditure over a certain sum.

Manley decided that the man to convince was Don McAllister. Don was visiting two factories during the next two weeks, and Bill made up his mind that if necessary he would cancel all appointments, travel with McAllister, and win him over.

Hugh was not deeply concerned. He wanted the position, but was quite happy to go along as personnel director. However, he was delighted to know that the other three directors would be willing to work under him – although he had no thought of mentioning this fact to Roland Huntley.

So each of the directors made his decision on facts, and benefits to the company and themselves. But with the exception of Hugh Fairley they had overlooked the fact that their own emotional personal involvement had coloured their thinking.

12 Motivating through Public Speaking

The Huntley Group had two training centres. At head office were three conference rooms, each capable of holding up to thirty people, with separate rooms for syndicate work. At Banbury in Oxfordshire, a manor house had been converted into a residential training centre for courses of five days or longer. Some were of a month's duration.

From all over the world Huntley employees travelled to Banbury to be updated in technical improvements, servicing, marketing, and all aspects of management. Public speaking courses, however, were always held in the conference rooms at headquarters.

Each room had a different décor, but all verged on the luxurious with deep carpets and well-upholstered chairs.

The directors had arrived separately, having previously agreed not to sit together. The fifteen other delegates, all managers within the group, had been told in advance that the main board directors were attending as an example to those many managers who were reluctant to participate in public speaking courses.

Tom Lawson had begun the campaign by sending out a memorandum entitled *Public Speaking as a Motivating Force* to all managers throughout the group. Although the pre-course instructors had made it clear that informal clothes were in order all fifteen managers, conscious of the occasion, were smartly dressed. They all wanted to create a good impression.

At two minutes to nine a course administrator entered the room and asked the delegates to take their seats. Strangely, the managers were not at all concerned that the top brass were present. They were now much more concerned with their own fears – the fear of making fools of themselves when it came to their turn to speak on the platform.

In the class, as well as the main board directors there were one managing director, two regional directors, and twelve divisional managers.

Sharply at nine o'clock training manager Timothy Currie entered the room and walked purposefully towards the desk at the centre of the platform.

The managers saw a man of medium height and sturdily built. They listened to his rich brown voice when he began, "Good morning, ladies and gentlemen. Let me first put your minds at rest and discuss your main fear – the fear of not acquitting yourself well when it is your turn to put the lessons learned into practice. I assure you that no one will be made to look foolish. Then there is the fear of the mind going blank in the middle of a speech."

He looked at them, and smiled. "Yes, it does happen on occasion. It has certainly happened to me, as it does to most speakers who are not glued to notes. But it doesn't matter. There need be no loss of dignity, no heart palpitation. I shall tell you how easy it is to overcome this fear."

Everyone relaxed a little.

Currie then said to one of the managers, "Kate, what did you have for breakfast this morning?"

Kate replied quite easily, and in some detail.

Turning to another manager he said, "Simon, if you were to win a top prize – say a million pounds in a football pool – what would be your first three priorities?"

Simon hesitated for only a moment, then said, "First, a bigger house."

"Why?" asked Currie.

Simon explained that the children were growing up and they really required more space to enable them to entertain their friends if necessary.

His next priority was a boat, as he was very keen on sailing. Then thirdly, a holiday for the whole family, to think what they should do with the rest of the money.

Currie turned to the audience and said, "Both Kate and Simon spoke easily and fluently, didn't they? No problem there at all! Now let me put another question to both of you – and maybe I'm speaking for real, this time; if I were to ask each of you to come up to the platform now and tell our managers in far more detail about your early morning activities, or about what you would do if you won the pools – if I asked you to speak for five minutes or more, would you like to do that, right *now?*" He raised his voice on the word *now*.

Everyone chuckled. Kate and Simon didn't budge, because they didn't know whether they had been given an instruction or not.

"Well?" asked Currie.

Kate said, "Well – yes – but . . ."

Simon had gone a pale green.

Currie said, "Don't worry. Neither of you is going to have to make a speech so early in the proceedings. But tell me this, both of you: when I first spoke to you about early morning breakfast, and the pools, you didn't have any racing heart beats, you weren't deeply concerned. We were just having a chat – nothing out of the ordinary. But when I made the request that you come to the platform and stand in front of everyone didn't your hearts palpitate a little? Didn't your hands sweat a little? Didn't your mind perhaps go blank?"

Simon said, "Yes, my mind did go blank for the moment – when you shouted *now*."

"Good! But before you make a complete recovery, just imagine this: the door opens now, and a course administrator enters and hands me a note. It is a directive from

Roland Huntley, telling you, Simon, and you, Kate, that he is indisposed and cannot address the audience of five thousand this evening at the Albert Hall at a BIM Conference. You both have to take his place, and all the audience want to hear from you is what you had for breakfast, Kate, and how you, Simon, would spend a fortune. Now how would you feel about that? Imagine the scene: five thousand executives staring at you, waiting for you to speak, wondering how you will perform . . . Now be honest, the truth please, Kate and Simon, how do you feel?"

"I'd collapse," said Simon.

Everyone laughed in a nervous sort of way, not being sure what Currie's next request would be.

"But why?" went on Currie. "Why is it so easy for Kate and Simon to have a chat with me from the comfort of their chairs, be slightly shocked to be invited to come up to the platform; while the thought of addressing five thousand people sets the nerve ends tingling and fear clouding their minds?

"The reason is that speaking in public is quite un-natural to the majority of people, and whatever we do that is not natural to us causes tension. If you talk to your own group of employees – and you do that regularly – there isn't much tension involved, but with a large auditorium such as the Albert Hall and, perhaps, a critical audience, everything changes. The thought of making a speech on an occasion like that makes even tough, hard-bitten executives' stomachs churn over for days in advance. The same applies if you have to speak under the watchful eyes of family and friends at a wedding. Such speeches have spoiled the enjoyment of a wedding for many a father, bridegroom, or whoever has to make a speech. When the moment arrives for you to stand on your feet, in spite of the fact that you have rehearsed, and rehearsed, and rehearsed, in spite of the fact that you have a handful of notes, the typewritten words become a hazy mist, merging into each other; the mind is in a turmoil.

"Some, faced with this terror, lose their heads, cast their notes aside and think they are being very strong when they say their wife wrote the notes or something similar, and they can't read them; or, to hell with the notes, let me talk as I feel. The result, nine times out of ten, is dreadful.

"Well, how are you all feeling now?"

Laughter eased the tension.

"Let me repeat, whenever we are asked to do something which is not quite natural to us, we become nervous. As I asked Simon to come up to the platform, his mind went temporarily blank. Why?

"This is how it was explained to me some years ago by an eminent consultant psychologist from the Tavistock Clinic; he, of course, used medical terms which I was unable to memorise, but this is roughly what he said in answer to my question as to what caused such fear to grow and grow in those who are under no physical threat and only have to speak in public:

"'Shock waves pass through the body. You need not concern yourselves how these are generated or how the muscles or the blood are affected. The end result is always a clouded mind.

"'Take, for example, a learner-driver about to take a test. He is not afraid physically of what might happen – but he is afraid of failure through making a mistake. Tension again builds on tension. The Highway Code which was once so clear in his mind fades away. Tension causes driving errors, which cause even more tension – and more driving errors . . . And so the learner-driver, so skilled when driving with his own instructor, is faced with failure when under test.'

"The same applies to public speaking, often with the same results – failure – because, as I mentioned earlier, public speaking, like taking driving tests, does not come naturally. Most managers rarely have to speak in public more than three or four times a year, and that isn't enough to gain experience or to overcome tension.

"It's not the same in the acting profession. Tension builds up for actors, but because they are professional performers this tension eases immediately they face the audience. This doesn't happen to the amateur public speaker.

"There are two ways to overcome the nervous tension which is suffered by so many public speakers: the first is the obvious one. Learn to relax, because the opposite of tension is relaxation, and I will talk about that in a few moments. The second is to speak on every possible occasion. Whenever you are invited to address an audience, whether it be ten or one hundred, do it. The experience itself will help you to overcome your tension. It will not, necessarily, help you to become a good speaker, but it will help to steady your nerves when the speaking begins. Few of you, however, will take this advice, and there is, in fact, an easier and better way.

"I shall give you a series of simple exercises to help you to become a more relaxed person. You will find that in a few days you will achieve *some* benefit and *great* benefit in about four months.

"There is much talk, these days, about the need for managers to have regular checks on their health. I'm not in the health business, but if you do become a more relaxed person, then surely your health will benefit.

"However, the only reason we have introduced these relaxation exercises is to help you to become a more effective public speaker. I asked my friend at the Tavistock Clinic how I could become a more relaxed person, and how I could teach others to relax. I told him that I had read many books on the subject and had listened to experts on radio and television, but although there was nothing wrong with any of their solutions to the problem, they didn't work for me. Some advised breathing exercises; others suggested sitting on the floor cross-legged deep in meditation.

"My friend explained to me that in order to relax completely one needed a trouble-free mind – and that was where most relaxation exercises failed.

"The advice given usually is to lie on a bed every day, or sit quietly in a chair and empty the mind; followed by exercises involving the mind and body. But this is quite impossible for the average person. He or she cannot empty the mind and think of nothing at all, to order. Under these conditions they can only think of their problems – and it is the problems which are causing the tension. Yet it is not possible for the mind to influence the muscles of the body to relax if there is no concentration of thought.

"I then asked my friend about meditation, to which he replied, 'Wonderful! But deep meditation can only be mastered by relatively few people – at least, in this country. I have no great knowledge of what happens in India, where the gurus are able to meditate for hours. In this country deep meditation is often the last resort of the neurotic, and it rarely helps.' Then he added, 'I believe the answer lies in the mind not being blank, but filled with a key word or words which can influence the muscles of the body to relax. It is the relaxation of the muscles which influences the mind – and it is the mind which influences the muscles'."

Currie paused for a moment and said, "And that was about all from my friendly psychologist, but from that advice we have developed what we call *the one-minute relaxation technique*. It works and, in fact, it cannot fail if you carry out the special exercises every day. Do this and you will never again be overcome by such tension as to stop you from giving of your best, whatever the situation.

"In the same way as a golfer can only concentrate his thoughts on one tiny aspect of his swing at a time (never the complete swing) so, to relax your body, you cannot succeed by thinking of your whole body. The brain can't cope with that thought, because it cannot define the complete body, for the purposes of relaxing.

"Relaxing must become a habit, and the way to form that habit is to achieve success quickly. The *minute* technique doesn't allow for the introduction of negative thoughts; and during this short period you *can* concentrate on one section of your body. Most people can concentrate their minds for one minute at a time and that's all that is required, to begin our relaxing programme.

"Here are the sections:

Your left arm and shoulder muscles
your right arm and shoulder muscles
your left leg muscles
your right leg muscles
your stomach and chest muscles
your back muscles
your face muscles.

"Think for a moment of your left arm: that's easy enough, isn't it? Before concentrating on your muscles, however, there are two words that you have to remember. If you tell yourself to relax that doesn't seem to have much effect, but if you tell a muscle or any part of your body to *let go*, after a short while those muscles will do just that – they will let themselves go. As a standard expression, when anyone is tense we often say to them, 'For Goodness' sake let yourself go!'

"So far, then, you only have to remember seven parts of your body and two words: *let go*.

"For one minute only, concentrate all your thoughts on the muscles of your left arm and shoulder. Don't worry about the rest of your body – only the left arm and shoulder. First tense these muscles, then quietly say to them, *let go*. Say the word *let* as you breathe in, and *go* as you breathe out.

"Continue this one-minute exercise for seven days. Never try to succeed more quickly by lengthening the time. You will know when your muscles are relaxed when you get a warm, tingling feeling in your left arm and shoulder only.

"During the second week, concentrate your thoughts on your right arm and shoulder. Think about them for one minute at a time two or three times a day, as well as when you go to bed. *Forget all about your left arm and shoulder, which will now relax automatically.*

"In the third week you must carry out the same procedure with your left leg. For this purpose, you must be sitting down or lying on your bed. When you sit, do *not* cross your legs – place your feet flat on the ground.

"Concentrate, during the fourth week, on your right leg, forgetting all about your arms and your left leg.

"Think about your stomach and chest during the fifth week.

"During the sixth week it is the turn of your back.

"Finally, in the seventh week you will concentrate on your facial muscles. You must not clench your teeth and there must be no wrinkles on your forehead.

"Assuming you have made good progress, you will be relaxing completely within seven weeks, and for the following two or three months you will be able to concentrate all your thoughts on your facial muscles, and your other muscles will automatically relax.

"Under stress you will take each part of your body in turn. For example, if you can't get to sleep, don't count sheep; just start on your left arm and shoulder, and move from section to section of your body. Long before you reach your facial muscles you will probably be fast asleep.

"After six months have gone by – and not before – you can try to relax for longer than one minute at a time, until gradually you have increased the time to as long as you wish. You will find you can definitely relax for half an hour or so; but don't expect miracles during the first weeks, although there will be some immediate benefits. Then, it will all happen quickly.

"So here, again, are the rules you need. It will help you to remember them if you write them down – and I'll dictate slowly:

"One, remember seven parts of the body:

> the left arm and shoulder
> the right arm and shoulder
> the left leg
> the right leg
> the stomach and chest
> the back
> the face

"And remember the words: *let go*.

"Now, start with the left arm and shoulder. Tell the muscles to *let go*. Keep repeating this for one minute. Do it tonight when you go to bed, and then repeat this exercise two or three times a day. Concentrate on this left arm and shoulder only for the first seven days.

"After seven to ten days you can repeat this exercise on your right arm and shoulder – *forgetting your left arm* – and carry on with this for the next seven to ten days.

"Concentrate in turn on the remaining five parts of your body – seven to ten days on each part.

"After two or three months, continue this *let go* procedure with the facial muscles.

"After six months of practising, increase the time to between two and five minutes for each period.

"Remember to keep up these short daily relaxing exercises until your muscles respond automatically at the least sign of tension.

"Now for some *don'ts*:

"*Don't* try to relax your whole body while sitting down. Just rest your arms on your uncrossed legs and concentrate on relaxing your arms and legs only.

"*Don't* wrinkle your forehead, or tightly close your eyelids or mouth while relaxing your facial muscles."

Currie paused and looked around at his audience and then said, "And that's all you need to know to enable you to acquire the habit of relaxing. What we are going to do now is to begin the exercises, and we'll take each part of the body in turn – although when you start these exercises properly tonight you will begin only with the left arm and shoulder.

"There is of course an exception – one person who has no need of the *let go* technique. He is the thick-headed speaker who honestly believes he is perfect. He never suffers from nerves, and he glories in being asked to speak.

"This type of man was exemplified in an article I read in the *Daily Mail* by a journalist, Lynda Lee-Potter. I'll read it to you:

". . . 'I write as somebody who has sat next to more provincial after-banquet-speaking mayors than most, eating their own roast chicken dinners and mine, untroubled by any hint of insecurity, any qualm of unease and saying *Never had no troubles with MY nerves little lady*.

"'They then stand up with total aplomb, impressive éclat, without one little cloud of self doubt spoiling their evening, and proceed to wreck it for everybody else by giving a performance of sleep-inducing torpidity'."

After they had practised the relaxing exercises several times Currie announced a break for coffee.

On recommencing after the coffee break Currie said, "I was glad to see the bosses all relaxing so well." The general laughter included the bosses, and Currie let them all settle down again before carrying on.

"Our main board executives here have set us all a fine example, and I am sure that, from now on, every manager in the company will be queueing up to attend our public speaking courses. You have all met Don McAllister who is carrying out an across the board consultancy assignment. I know some of you were a little sceptical at first, but I am sure that you have now all been won over by the ability and consideration shown by his consultants.

"I have asked Don to come up on to the platform – after all, he's used to public speaking so I'm sure he won't be at all tense – to talk to us about public speaking in the United States of America."

McAllister left his chair at a signal from Currie, and made his way to the platform as the instructor stepped down and joined the managers.

McAllister began, "It's true what you said, Tim, we all do get the jitters from time to time, but as far as I'm concerned I lose them the minute I get to my feet. And I'm sure that in the future this is going to apply to all the managers here.

"May I begin by giving you some figures. No one can dispute them – and I can't prove them. When we consider all the various business functions, dinners and conferences that we attend, I don't think we hear possibly ten good speakers out of a hundred – and I'm talking now about the USA, not Great Britain. We have the same number of mumblers, shouters, bores, and colourless speakers as you do. While over here I have seen and heard on television men who are running the affairs of associations, who speak for the British business-man, and politicians who are supposed to speak for everyone. Few of them are articulate; few of them can hold our attention for long.

"When you, as managers, address meetings, your objective is nearly always to motivate your audience to do something better – to sell better, produce more, build a better team spirit, agree to changes, undertake new projects or even to give cash to charities. It is Tim Currie's job to motivate you to become better public speakers. He has already shown you how to relax. Has he motivated you enough? He certainly has motivated me! I'm going to start this evening and continue every day and, as he has suggested, even for a few minutes while sitting down during the day, I shall try to concentrate on relaxing.

"To motivate you to spend some of your time to become better public speakers is a difficult task, because unfortunately even the highly nervous among you believes he already acquits himself quite well. Don't be cross with me; remember, in my view, one in ten good speakers would be about average. You can't be honest with yourselves, because you don't know – and even your best friends won't tell you the truth. Will those of you who have been bored or annoyed by speakers during the last few months put up your hands?"

Nearly everyone waved back at him.

McAllister continued, "But all the speakers you heard thought they were brilliant! Why? Because of the politeness and good manners of their associates and friends. When those speakers sat down to applause – and we all applaud the bad as well as the good, again out of politeness – they felt they had acquitted themselves well. And this surely had been proved by the Chairman when he whispered, 'Well done!' If the speaker happens to be a high ranking politician, or a chief executive, the position worsens. All the sycophants will be hypocritical and will congratulate him in an overgenerous manner, so that when he returns home he will tell his wife how well he had performed – and he will then go on boring others for ever.

"Recently I watched an Actor-of-the-Year award which was also being filmed for television. There were three speakers, plus the winner of the award. The speakers were a well-known comedian, an equally well-known script writer, and an actress. Only the actress spoke well. The others, in spite of humorous stories, and general laughter at very poor stories, were bad – extremely bad. I was sitting at a table for ten, and throughout the stories all I heard was 'Dreadful!', 'Oh do shut up!', 'You've told that one at least a dozen times!' and other, equally critical remarks. Yet, when each of the speakers sat down, all ten of us clapped as if we had just heard a Churchillian oration. And although these were professionals, they had not learned the art of speaking in public – only how to speak from scripts or to write scripts. There was too much repetition, too many attempts at humour, and every speech was too long. Of course, there are some great speakers, and we all enjoy listening to them. But great speakers invariably keep to the rules. It is only the incompetent ones who believe that they can be successful by breaking the rules.

"Of course, you will always have the ranters, who are enjoyed by the audiences – but these audiences have come to hear them rant. They are not public speakers, they are actors, playing ranting parts.

"May I now make a suggestion? Let us all believe that we are not good speakers in spite of all the praise we may have received in the past. Let us all become better speakers because we have gone to the trouble of coming here, to receive help in mastering the art. Let us abide by Tim Currie's rules, and I am sure that if we keep to those rules we shall receive – and deserve – praise, not flattery."

Don McAllister left the platform amidst prolonged applause. As he reached his chair someone shouted out, "And that's not flattery!"

When Tim was once more on the platform he said, "Thank you, Don. I'm sure most of us will still go on misleading ourselves in the future but we'll try to be more objective."

Then straightening his shoulders he went on, "To-day is *input* day. I shall do most of the talking, and you will do most of the listening. But on Tuesday and Wednesday you will do most of the talking, and I shall be the listener. Before we can think of speech building, and voice production, however, we have to think what immediate effect we are likely to have on an audience. I am sure you will all agree that first impressions of a speaker do influence our minds.

"If he is wearing a suit apparently bought from Oxfam and two sizes too large for him, the minds of his audience will be concentrating on his clothes, rather than on his opening words. No one ever gets a second chance to make a good first impression. The collective minds of the audience can be motivated, not only by a speaker's appearance, but even by the way he walks on to the platform.

"The rule is quite simple: dress for the occasion, and always walk with a purposeful air. Don't slink, don't rush, don't strut, but take firm steps. You have made a good entrance, and you are about to speak. But first, here are some rules for after-dinner speakers:

"Prior to speaking don't keep dabbing at your mouth with your table napkin. The audience will already have begun to look at you and dislike such irritating habits. Another habit to avoid is nose blowing. Too many speakers blow their nose two or three times – presumably, it's a form of release of nervous tension.

"Don't keep drinking before you rise and don't take a final drink, whether it be water or wine, before you begin your speech.

"Don't leap from your chair on being announced, as if a mouse had run up your leg; but don't take so long to get to your feet that the audience begin to wonder if you are chained to your chair.

"Never start by waving your hands about. If you do, you will continue to be a hand waver throughout the speech. I'm sure it drives you to distraction when you see TV speakers making the same gestures time and time again for no apparent reason. And so, to begin with, you are faced with one of the speaker's greatest challenges: what to do with your hands and arms. Many solve the problem by making use of their hands as if they were flags to be waved – and nothing is more disconcerting to an audience than a flag waver, except, perhaps, continual outstretching of arms, as if appealing for help.

"The answer is simple. You can rest your hands on the table for a while – but if you do, do not sway backwards and forwards. For a change, you can clasp your hands in front of you or behind your back, using them only to colour or emphasise a salient feature of your speech.

"For example, if you are talking about world-wide exports you can with a circular arm movement depict the world as a whole. If you are showing strength and determination to achieve an objective, there is no harm in punching the air. You can point to the sky if you are talking about the achievements of one of your stars. You can pretend to smoke, or you can pretend to drink, so long as the movement makes sense to the audience, because it emphasises a point that you are making.

"The classic example referred to by every teacher of public speaking is to explain to the audience the shape of a spiral staircase. No amount of talking can achieve the same results as a movement of the hand and arm.

"The hands, then, are only used to add a pictorial element to a telling phrase. When you are on the platform tomorrow, concentrate your minds on this aspect of public speaking. Don't cause distraction in your performance by repetitive hand waving, or other inadvisable movements which may prevent the audience concentrating on your words.

"Now, from the hands we move on to other mannerisms which irritate audiences. You have all, at some time, felt like shouting out 'Don't keep doing that!' – tapping the desk, scratching a chin, or playing with a piece of crayon . . .

"May I have some of your pet hates now please, and we'll try to find the worst hate of all. They come under two headings: *physical* and *verbal*. Let us begin with the physical.

"The *throat clearer* was the first response.

"Right!" said Currie. "He does annoy us, doesn't he? But I do want to emphasise a point: mannerisms only irritate if they are repetitive. An occasional clearance of the throat once or twice during a speech is not a mannerism. Off we go again."

The audience reacted quickly. *Fidgeting, nose pulling, ceiling gazing, glancing at a watch* . . . . . There were many others, but they all decided that the worst offender of all was the speaker who was never still but kept moving the whole time – the *fidget*; and they solemnly agreed never to fidget again.

"Except," said Currie with a smile, "when you start talking tomorrow when that vow can be so easily broken." Then he added, "But now let us consider the type of speaker we hate listening to. Your pet bores, please?"

Later, he summarised all of them by writing their names on the white board.

"The *Asider* – who seems to reserve his best quips for those sitting alongside him.

"The *Monosyllabler* – a word, a pause; two words, two pauses . . . More pauses than words.

"The *Statue* – the rigid speaker who is, apparently, encased in plaster. He always looks as if he is talking down at us.

"The *Pompous* – he makes us feel that he is doing us a great favour by speaking to us at all.

"The *Emotionalist.* A little emotion is good; it shows that the speaker has a heart and feelings; but the true emotionalist emotes all the time. He is either crying, ranting, or shouting, in his plea to us to join him in his objective. At first, we like him. Then we see through him. And then we go off him.

"The *Funny Man* – very few comedians, even the best, can make us laugh for twenty minutes. Often they hardly make us laugh at all – and they have script writers to back them up! But the funny-man public speaker believes that he can do better than the professionals and make us laugh, and laugh, and laugh . . . One or two stories do add colour, but a stream of jokes always leads to failure.

"The *Starer* – he won't give everyone a chance to feel that he is speaking to them. He fixes his gaze on one person in the front row, and looks at him all the time, apparently always speaking to him – much to the discomfort of that one person.

"The *Whisperer* – 'I can't hear you' cries out a member of the audience, but the whisperer goes on whispering. He isn't addressing those at the back of the room – that's one of the reasons why he isn't heard. We can hardly hear him, even when he uses a microphone."

This list completed, Currie said, "Before we break for lunch, we shall now think of all those phrases and sentences that we dislike so much when they are repeated continually. Your views please?"

Those most disliked by the managers were:

The point is . . .
To put it plainly . . .
As I was saying . . .
That reminds me . . .
Well . . .
Look . . .
So . . .
Call to mind . . .
The long and short of it . . .
By and large . . .
If I may say so . . .
In my humble opinion . . .
And, of course, ahs and ums – and ers . . .

The list completed, Currie said, "Well, in my humble opinion we should now stop for lunch."

The afternoon session was taken by Alan Batey, known throughout the group as the man with the golden voice. Batey was always in great demand as an after-dinner speaker. Few could match the quality of his voice, his command of the English language, and his fluency. A plumpish man with thick black hair, he looked the actor he once was.

After introducing himself and explaining his position in the group he said, "Tim will soon be telling you about the techniques of speech building. If, however, a speaker cannot be heard clearly, hasn't an attractive voice, and cannot hold your attention by his diction and use of language, then the subject matter of his speech won't be of any great importance. The audience will soon stop listening and allow their minds to dwell on other things.

"That doesn't mean that he must possess the voice of a Burton or a Gielgud, but it does mean that it shouldn't be harsh, grating, toneless, or lack-lustre. This afternoon I want to talk to you about the voice, and how the quality can be improved by a few simple exercises.

"We'll begin with voice production. Voice production is based on good breathing, and good breathing means controlled breathing, or taking in the right amount of breath at the right place, and using it in order to give the right motive power that makes for voice quality. Everyone has the machinery for this control, and when that machinery is not used properly, we lack breath. This results in irregular rhythm and poor voice quality.

"Most people, when attempting to put more power into their voice, think of their vocal chords. This only causes tension in the muscles surrounding the vocal chords, resulting in a dry, wheezy tone of voice. To improve your voice quality you must forget your vocal chords and concentrate on your lungs. You will then have taken your first step towards diaphragmatic breathing.

"Unfortunately, natural breathing sometimes means taking in only shallow breaths. If we are called on to make a speech, this results in quickly running out of breath – perhaps feeling unwell, or just managing to stutter and stammer our way through the ordeal.

"Now we're going to carry out a test. Place the palm of your hand firmly on that V-shape in the breastbone, just below the rib. You can feel the diaphragm working gently. Imagine that you have raced round the block and are puffing hard. Now all puff together – you can feel the diaphragm working really hard, can't you?

"This is what is happening. As you inhale your lungs expand, pushing the elastic diaphragm down and out. As you exhale, in and up goes the diaphragm, resulting in more rapid propulsion of the outgoing air passing over the vocal chords. When you speak you inhale more rapidly and exhale more slowly. This enables you to conserve your breath to make words and sentences. Well done!

"Now for another test. Imagine that you have just enjoyed a wonderful meal prepared by a cordon bleu chef, with specially selected vintage wines. You are the guest of honour and your virtues have been extolled. You've made your speech, and received warm and generous applause. Now you sit back in your chair feeling that all is well with the world.

"You sigh a sigh of deep repletion and contentment. Have you got the picture?

"Right! Now sigh – sigh deeply. And once more . . . How deeply you breathed!

"That sigh exercise is, basically, all that you need to know about breath replenishment.

"You did all sigh beautifully! Let us do it again. And now for the third test. All breath, when correctly used, should enter through the nostrils, to filter and warm it. But occasionally this may be noisy, and not instantaneous in its effect. For silence and efficiency, therefore, breath may be taken in through a slightly open mouth.

"Now breathe in through your mouth while it is only slightly open. When you have reached what you believe to be the absolute limit of expansion of the diaphragm, take in a little more breath and there will be more expansion.

"Now try once more – there is always some room left for expansion. Conversely, when you believe you have emptied your lungs of air there is nearly always some breath left in the lungs – some energy left in the diaphragm, to give the air that extra propulsion. This enables you, when necessary, to speak long sentences without taking breath, resulting in a smooth vocal tone, without jerkiness.

"The next exercise we can consider will help you to gain effective breath control. Will you please all stand up." There ensued a general shuffling of feet as the audience complied with the request.

"Breathe deeply," he said. "Most people raise their shoulders as they take deep breaths, but this action doesn't help your breathing at all. Count five as you breathe in; and then, as you start to breathe out, count to ten, increasing gradually to twenty. If you repeat this exercise six times daily it will help to develop your breath control.

"Let's now try something different: to maintain correct breathing, but to put a lilt into your voice, you should sing."

Alan Batey moved amongst the managers, pressing down shoulders. "We are going to sing. What shall we sing? How about a snatch of 'Land of Hope and Glory'? I'll conduct."

They all sang enthusiastically, and during the song Alan Batey stopped continually, changing from singing to speaking. They all noticed that singing resulted in the following spoken sentence sounding more mellow and tuneful.

Batey told them to carry out this exercise daily. "My final advice," he went on, "is to practise reading aloud from a book, to improve your rhythm."

His next subject was the formation of words.

He began, "When we say 'he's tongue-tied' we usually mean that someone doesn't communicate very well. But speakers in every category often become tongue-tied in a different sense. They don't realise that the tongue is meant to move into position, in order to establish sounds accurately.

"A lively tongue must work in conjunction with a mobile jaw, to give clarity to the words we use. Few speakers open their mouths wide enough, and this must result in an imperfect and muffled tone. You can't speak effectively through half-closed lips. The answer is: yawn. That's easy enough, isn't it? Yawn six times. It will help you to have a more mobile jaw.

"Repeat six times *you*, *why*, and *Yokohama*, exaggerating each word as you say it. Carry out this exercise morning and evening – it works wonders.

"To make your tongue more mobile, place a finger about one inch away in front of your mouth, and try to touch that finger with your tongue. Do it now!"

They did.

"Move the finger a little further away and try again. Now keep your tongue straight and try imitating a snake, by flicking out your tongue and trying to reach your finger.

"Try touching the tip of your nose with your tongue.

"Repeat these exercises six times every day.

"Now, let us, together, try to improve our diction. Many a time you must have wondered if, perhaps, your hearing was impaired, when listening to an after-dinner speaker. We now know that this lack of clarity may be due to many factors.

"It can, however, happen even when a speaker is

shouting, because the outline of his words may be blurred. It can be corrected by the better use of certain sounds – consonants like P T D CH K L M N give greater emphasis and sharper authority to the words we use.

"Have you heard of *Slurvian?* Another Ruritanian kingdom? Not at all! It is the language of those who slur their words.

"Here are some examples:

Lazn'genlmn   instead of   ladies and gentlemen
Awnjuice   instead of   orange juice
azamarrafac'   instead of   as a matter of fact

"The ts have disappeared and also a d in the first example, and an r in the second.

"*Slurvian* must be avoided at all costs.

"Now let us think, for a moment, about the vowel sounds. Consonants are standard, but vowel sounds can change the type of speech we use. We all remember a e i o u but, of course, there are many other vowel sounds. Effective vowel use is achieved by the elasticity of the lips. Without this flexibility we are apt to say *terdye* instead of today, feller instead of fellow, and ejicate instead of educate.

"Here is an exercise for you to practise at home in front of a mirror. Whisper a e i o u, and watch your lips moving. Repeat the exercise a little louder, still watching the lip movements. Then shout out the sounds.

"You will *see* your lips moving. Next, mouth the vowels without making a sound. Exaggerate the effort and watch the lip movements, all the time.

"Repeat this exercise six times."

Alan then returned to the beginning and went through each exercise again. He explained that success could only come from constant practice. He then showed how, by applying these exercises, the great public speaking sin of sounding monotonous could be eradicated. He explained how some words should be emphasised, for effect; that slang should be avoided; his concluding words were, "Colourful delivery is the expression of a vibrant personality."

They broke, then, for tea, and fifteen minutes later, Tim Currie began the next session by summarising the day's work.

"One," he said, "a good speaker motivates. Two, a speech is vastly improved when the speaker is relaxed. Three, we switch off when we can't hear a speaker clearly and he has a monotonous voice that lulls us to sleep.

"Now let us look at the structure of speech." For the ensuing thirty minutes Currie explained that there had to be research in depth before even the shortest speech.

"Long before you begin to write your speech you must, first, ask yourself these questions:

"Why should they want to listen to me?
"How will they benefit from listening to me?
"What is the objective of my speech?
"How do I persuade and motivate?
"How can I inspire?

"Then, you must ensure that you have all the facts right; that you know what the audience expects of you; that you have several anecdotes and quotations to choose from and to build into your speech; and that you have, perhaps, stories to tell which involve some members of the audience, which is always a sure winner.

"Also, you must consider the length of the speech – and whatever length you decide upon, cut it by a third or a half. Nine speeches out of ten are too long. If the convenor of the meeting asks you to talk for an hour, tell him that you are only willing to talk for half an hour, but that if an hour has to be filled you can cover the extra thirty minutes by answering questions. If you are making an informal after-dinner speech, five minutes is usually long enough.

"It may be heartbreaking to take out some of those special stories – one or two of the highlights – but if you were to employ an editor, that is what he would do and the speech would be all the better for it."

Currie then emphasised that no one should ever make an impromptu speech. If a request is even remotely possible, you should be prepared and have a 'filler' speech ready. It may be a little disappointing if you are not called upon, but it's much more disappointing to make a bad impromptu speech.

"Now, back again to speech building. You'll have carried out your research. You'll have accumulated your facts. You'll have built your speech, step by step; but go through it once more. Make certain that you're satisfied, then write it out in full from your notes.

"Having done that, don't read it again yourself, but get someone else to read it to you. You will, now, have to polish it up, and the best way for me to help you to do this is by taking each step and dealing with it separately. This I will do before dealing with the question of whether it is advisable to memorise your speech or to work from notes.

"These are the main points for you to remember in speech building:

"One, before preparing a speech: (a) think about it for several days; (b) research; (c) ask questions.

"Two, decide what kind of a speech you are going to make: (a) to impart information; (b) to persuade; (c) to inspire; (d) an after-dinner speech.

"Three, the main steps must be: the opening; creation of interest; the body of the speech (which can be subdivided into several steps); the close.

"Four, write down the main facts which will apply to each step.

"Five, cut out facts which are of little importance.

"Six, devise a good opening sentence for each fact.

"Seven, elaborate in this manner: (a) give statistics to prove a point; (b) present evidence to prove your point; (c) give an historical fact; (d) tell an anecdote; (e) tell a humorous story; (f) give an analogy; (g) give a quotation; (h) recite a poem, or a part of a poem. You need not use more than one, two, or three of these, and you can place them in any order.

"Eight, remember these rules: statistics – make them live; quotations – make them apt; anecdotes – bring yourself into the story."

Currie then paused, took a long drink of water, and went on: "Let's look at the main steps in greater detail. The first, you will remember, is the opening. What kind of an opening should we use?

"There are two rules to remember: first, never apologise by using such sentences as 'I'm not much good at this kind of thing . . .' 'I don't know why they asked me to speak' – never, never apologise. Secondly, start off on a low key. This doesn't mean mumbling, only lowering the tone of the voice a little to begin with. To start by shouting, or with a high-pitched appeal, may appear to be showmanship, but it doesn't work.

"These are the standard openings used, on occasion, by every speaker: I'll give them to you in no particular order – I'll start with an informal opening. Here are some examples:

" 'I was speaking to your chairman yesterday and he told me . . .' – low key, but always most acceptable. Everyone wants to know what the chairman has said.

"A good question opening takes some beating, if you want to get off to a good start. With a question opening always involve the audience, even if it is a rhetorical question to which no answer is expected – and most questions are rhetorical. For example: 'Have you heard of the Hepplewyth bird?' A pause, then, 'It always flies backwards, because it isn't interested in where it's going – only in where it has been. Are we like the Hepplewyth bird? Are we living in the past? . . .'

"And here is another example: Can you quickly work out what 3s 6d in the old monetary system is in terms of decimal currency?"

A pause again: everyone's mind is churning over. He went on, "Not very easy, is it, because we forget so quickly. Let me remind you . . ."

"Tomorrow you will all be asked to think of informal and question openings, as well as other openings – so listen carefully.

"One opening which I have used occasionally when I have reason to believe that an audience is against me, rather than with me, is the *mind-reading* opening. Here is an example: 'Let me begin by reading your thoughts. Ready? Good! You weren't keen to come here, were you? You're all very busy people and you probably thought it just another time-wasting ploy on the part of senior management. I'd feel the same in your place – but let me explain . . .'

"This form of opening always relaxes a difficult audience. It's a human approach, and it's usually a winner!

"A *humorous* opening is only successful if it can be linked to a personality in the room or, if the speech is to be made in an hotel, inefficiencies of the hotel staff. We've all been in situations when we have been ignored by a waiter, or a taxi driver has taken us the long way round, to run up a bill. If you can't turn an old story around – and most of the stories *are* old ones – to fit an occasion, then don't use a humorous opening. To open with a straightforward joke is nearly always a disaster.

"Then there is the *local colour* opening, which works wonders if you are speaking away from home. Your immediate reference to the vicinity, or the country – provided that you give honest praise and not flattery – invariably appeals to an audience, as it is taken as a tribute to those working in the area."

Currie paused, then said, "There are many, many more to come and later we shall go through all of them; but there is a limit to our time so we must concentrate on those which are used most often by professional speakers. But you can, if you wish, begin with an apt quotation or a reference to topical events, or you can hope to arouse curiosity with a story such as, 'I got home late the other evening and realised that I'd left my keys at the office. I was wondering what to do when this beautiful girl arrived and said –' We are all curious to know the outcome – if the story has a beginning, a middle, and an end and is short, it may well be the right beginning for that occasion.

"Finally, remember when opening, if you can use the word *you* then do it – and do it often. You will then be talking to the audience, and not at them. For example, 'You are all men and women who are well versed in farming. You will know, therefore . . .' Think of the audience – think of the word *you* – and then link them together."

There were then questions from the managers, which Currie handled well. Afterwards he concluded, "That's a brief review of openings, but remember, no sooner have you gripped the audience with your opening than you have to fight on to maintain their interest. Often, after a good opening, an audience relaxes. To achieve your objective, you must get quick *yes* responses from the audience. You must keep them thinking. Say something that will make the audience want to shout, 'You're one hundred per cent right!', 'That's what I believe!' or alternatively, 'You're wrong – completely wrong. It isn't true!'

"A controversial issue can quickly involve an audience – but you must know how you are going to win them over later. If you can get the audience to agree quickly, you will immediately maintain their interest.

"Another way of achieving interest is to give the

audience off-the-record information. We all like to be told about what went on at that famous party, or behind the scenes at the boardroom meetings, or on film location."

Currie sat on the edge of the table, surveyed the audience and said, "We have opened our speech: we have gripped our audience. What comes next? It is the *objective* of our speech, obviously, which incorporates audience benefits or facts – but included there must also be a *confidence builder*, if possible. And that should come quite early on.

"None of us is as famous as we think we are. You may, possibly, have been introduced by the chairman – but the audience will hardly have listened to him, anyway. Everyone will be eager to hear the main speaker, and if the chairman does eulogise you as a person, many of the audience may be sceptical – may even be put off you by the chairman's kindly remarks. If, therefore, you can work in a sentence early in your opening that will ease these very critical minds, you should do so. But don't do it blatantly.

"For example, we often hear someone saying, 'In all my fifty years' experience . . .' What does that mean? It could be bad experience – and it will date him, anyway. But you could say something like this: 'My six years under Professor LeRose taught me that . . .' or, 'When I worked on the production line – yes, I did, for five years – I was at that time always against those above me. Why? . . .' Another example: 'When I wrote *How to Succeed*, the first publishers I offered it to didn't like it and told me that it wouldn't be a successful seller. Now, that publisher must have sleepless nights thinking of all the profits he's lost from my last twenty books'.

"Even if you believe that your audience is aware of your background and that you have a right to address them, play safe, and add a confidence builder."

Currie concluded the session by announcing a five-minute break.

On recommencing Currie said, "We now come to the body of the speech and we have to remind ourselves of our objective: *to satisfy audience wants.*

"Whether they be left-wingers or right-wingers, ranters or ravers, or even quiet speakers, whether or not a speaker is talking complete nonsense . . . provided it is nonsense the audience wants to hear – provided the speaker satisfies their wants, the speech will go down well.

"Of course, a speaker on high technology will probably be talking to an audience eager to hear every word, but even he has to make his speech interesting. He must satisfy the wants of the audience in every respect if he is to be carefully listened to from the beginning of the speech to the end. Here are the main audience 'wants':

  to gain knowledge
  to achieve a better way of life
  to achieve pleasure and happiness
  to feel proud
  to gain something tangible – money, increased
    turnover, increased exports
  to benefit their health
  to be amused or entertained
  to consolidate their faith
  to enjoy the speaker's natural ability, whatever the
    subject – for example, a charitable appeal or an after
    dinner speech
  and finally, they want to be inspired.

"Think, then, of your main objective – and build your speech on that objective. Subsequently list, perhaps, twenty points which would benefit the audience. Check carefully, and then cut the twenty to perhaps ten – or even five – points, depending on the depth of explanation expected, or the length of the speech.

"If you concentrate on audience benefits – what will do

them good, what will please them, what will make them happy, what will make them charitable – you will, undoubtedly, evolve an excellent speech."

There followed a speech building exercise. Delegates were formed into syndicates, each syndicate having a different speech to consider, and each having to decide on ten points to satisfy audience wants.

After the delegates had returned, and the syndicate leaders had given the results and these results had been discussed, Currie said, "All that is now left for us to consider is the best ways of closing our speech.

"First, a rule – an unbreakable rule: Never give closing signals such as

And finally . . .
Before I sit down I must explain . . .
Now one last word . . .
I shall end with . . .

"Unfortunately, too many speakers do give these closing signals, but do not adhere to them. Suddenly, they remember yet another story and they go on, and on – and on . . . It's always fatal.

"But even if they do mean to close in a few seconds, when they mention the closing signals the audience relaxes; they put papers in folders, and switch off. Never give a closing signal; when you have finished, sit down quickly.

"Here are some of the ways in which you can close your speech:

Give a summary
Ask a question, so that the audience will be left pondering.
Be dramatic. Raise your voice to a crescendo, or lower your voice to a whisper, when making a final, dramatic appeal.
Close with an apt quotation.

Close by giving a concession: an invitation; a free book; extra commission or prizes . . . Offer a special service: a reduction in subscription, for example.
Use a story close – a good story with an unexpected ending always appeals and is bound to bring support.
Use a humorous story ending – but be careful of this one. It only works perhaps once in five times. Only if you have heard another speaker use it and bring the house down with it should you attempt it.
Close on an alternative – for example, you could say, 'Are we going to give way to this intimidation, or are we going to stand up and fight? It's up to you!' or 'Do you want your children to continue in this education system or do you want it changed? It is for you to make up your minds.'

"When the speech is finished, the congratulations (real or false!) are over and you return to your home or to your room, ask yourself these questions:

Did I really interest them or did I bore them?
Did I answer their questions satisfactorily?
Did I hold them all the way through the speech?
Did I speak enthusiastically, and clearly?

"You won't tell yourself the truth, but try to get as near to it as you can! Now, before we have a final break, I want to leave you with these golden rules: write down your speech; check it for interesting points; make certain that you have a good interest point at frequent intervals; see that the subject matter which builds up each step is interesting; check on your anecdotes and historical references, and your quotations; now, *cut your speech* and you are bound to be successful."

During the break Larry Duckworth commented to Don McAllister, "I can see now what crushingly boring speeches I must sometimes have made in the past."
Don answered, "Haven't we all!"

When the meeting recommenced the managers found a complete set of notes on their chairs. Then syndicates were formed, and each syndicate had to decide on six different closes, which were followed by general discussion.

Currie said, "What you now all want to know is how to remember your speech. This can be a speaker's greatest fear. Even if relaxed, a speaker can still be concerned at the thought of his mind going suddenly blank. You can all relax now – I'm going to give you the cure.

"The cure is to use *confidence cards*. First you have to think of the various ways a speaker must prepare his speech. He can:

write it out fully and read it
write it out fully and memorise it
write it out fully and refer to papers during the speech
write out notes to which he can refer during the speech
write it out fully, and memorise the headings.

"As we have already discussed, my advice is never to read a speech. But can you memorise it? If you have such a fine memory that you are able to do this you are a fortunate person, and you should be a good speaker. You will be able to polish every phrase, and having rehearsed it, you can deliver your speech effectively. However, few of us can do this. An actor might, although so often when making speeches actors tend to look as though they are acting, and you don't want to give that impression. But if you can memorise a whole speech, then make a good use of this blessing.

"How about writing it out fully, and continually referring to it? This can never be effective. To try to read each word from typewritten or handwritten pages, or even from a paper on which the words are printed in large letters, is most difficult. If you try this you will lose your place, become worried, and you will then make a bad speech.

"You can, of course, write notes, to which you can refer. This is quite normal procedure and often works well, provided the notes are legible and the speaker can understand them. But written words, the meaning of which was quite clear when we were preparing our speech, may mean nothing to us when we are actually on our feet, speaking.

"Finally we come to writing it out in full and then memorising the headings – and this, we have found, is easily the best policy for a speaker.

"Merely to write the headings is not sufficient – that is similar to making notes. The headings must convey to the speaker the step with which he is dealing, and the subject matter which he intends to use during that step.

"It can be achieved by writing out a good sentence to lead in to the step in the speech.

"Now for procedure: First write out your speech in full. Then seek out your key points – opening, creating interest, creating confidence, the individual steps in the body of the speech, the close. Underline the main sentences leading in to each of these key points.

"Now polish those sentences. Polish – and polish again . . . One of the reasons I advocate the sentence technique as against using headings as reminders is because it enables speakers to use scintillating sentences thought out in advance.

"Think about these key sentences. Develop them. You can, if you wish, also develop subsidiary sentences – sentences which will remind you of the next stage in the speech.

"So far, you have planned your speech. You have:

1 written it out in full
2 extracted your key sentences
3 polished your key sentences
4 memorised your key sentences
5 got the feel of the whole speech, because you have repeated it several times.

"Now you want to be certain that you won't forget a single factor of that speech. I believe you can take all the anxiety out of speech-making by using what we call *confidence cards*. Why cards? Cards are so simple to handle. They are easy to separate. They can be carried in a jacket pocket. They don't crumple easily. They can be held together by a ring if necessary. This is what you have to do:

"One, use as many cards as you have main steps or subsidiary steps in your speech.

"Two, divide each card into three sections. In the top left-hand section you will write your main sentence. On the top right-hand side you will have space for exhibits. Across the bottom you will have room for special points. And right in the top corner of the right-hand section you will number each card, so that they will look like this":

Currie drew on the white paper board:

MAIN SENTENCE	EXHIBITS	NO.
SPECIAL POINTS		

Turning back to the audience he continued, "In the left-hand section will be your main sentence for each of the steps. Now assuming that you may want to use a visual aid during this step – a magnet, a chart, even a glass of water – this will be written in the section headed *exhibits*. If there is any point that you want to be absolutely sure of elaborating during the step you can, under the third heading, make one or two further notes to which you can refer, or you can write a subsidiary sentence.

"And so you will continue, card after card, for each step – your main sentences, exhibits, special points, subsidiary sentences.

"Write on one side of the cards only, and write or print legibly. Before the speech commences, place your cards in front of you so that you can read them easily. Often you will find that you will make your whole speech without having to refer to the cards at all, but having them in front of you will give you great confidence."

Currie paused, then, pointing to the cards he had been using, he said, "I never speak without my cards."

Currie concluded the day's work saying, "Tomorrow you will all speak – and speak . . . and speak. You will see yourselves on video, but don't worry – by the time the day is over you will all be very pleased when you look at yourselves speaking.

"Your homework has been set for you. You will prepare your speeches including preparing some confidence cards ready for tomorrow's recordings. To begin with, no one will talk for more than two minutes. At the end of the day the time will be increased to five minutes. During the day we shall be constantly filming you and playing back the videos. In between, to give you all a break, we shall explain how to handle hecklers, how to lecture, how to use visual aids, how to use a microphone, and how to act as a chairman. Well, I said it was going to be a hard day. I was right, wasn't I?"

Fervently, they all agreed.

The days passed quickly. The managers, as Currie had promised, gained more and more confidence in themselves, and by the time Wednesday evening arrived they all wanted to carry on for another hour or so, making more speeches.

Currie's final words were, "We motivate by the words

we use and by our voices and actions. I hope you have all enjoyed being here, and that you have been motivated to plan and enjoy your public speaking in the future."

That evening the four directors and Don McAllister had dinner together in a small Italian restaurant nearby. They talked about the course, and all agreed that it was first-class, and well worth attending.

Don said, "We've nearly reached the end of our journey. There are only two more meetings, one for *time management*, and the other for *delegating*."

"I think we can leave out time management," said Fairley. "As you know, my team have been carrying out a survey on the subject. We've sent out questionnaires, and have had many interviews. I believe we should be wasting our time to discuss it further, because I think I can put before you all the fundamental information that you require. Would a memorandum on the subject from me, covering our survey, be sufficient?"

Everyone readily agreed. The meetings had taken up so much of their time during the previous months.

Hugh Fairley said, "The final meeting, then, on delegating, should take place at my house. It's my turn."

This, too, was agreed.

Over coffee McAllister said, "Our consultancy work for your group is nearly over, and we have discovered very little wrong: but the report will cover the whole spectrum of Huntley activities. Possibly, the weakest link – and I mention this now – is lack of innovation over the last two years."

Manley began to protest, but McAllister went on, "You needn't protest, Bill – I must congratulate you!"

Manley looked expectantly at the consultant.

"You have worked wonders at your factories," McAllister continued, "and the team spirit is really good, you've overcome all the early problems. During the last twelve months you have introduced a magazine for the factory employees. I can tell you now that it is read – it isn't just a company publicity sheet, you include many controversial articles in it. I know that the publication comes under Hugh's auspices but you provide much of the material, and it was your idea, originally. You have open days each month, when workers can bring their families to have production methods explained to them. You'd think no one would be interested, but they are! They all turn up, and you give them a good meal afterwards, in the canteen."

"That's why they turn up," said Bill with a laugh.

"That isn't true, and they also appreciate the fact that you have used space for playgrounds and crèches for the children, with a nurse in attendance for when part-time workers have to bring their children with them. You walk the floors, and insist that every senior manager does the same – and every director visiting one of your factories has to do a walkabout, like it or not! There isn't anything we can teach you, Bill, about communication."

Manley said, "Thank you for that, but I'm afraid you have exaggerated a little. The whole board has been involved in creating a better family spirit."

"Good!" said Don. "So now you won't mind the criticism I have made in the report about lack of innovation."

"I'll argue, just the same," said Manley.

"I'm sure you will!" McAllister then concluded, "You're a first class board of directors, and I've enjoyed working with you."

It was then the directors' turn to thank McAllister – and on that happy note, the meeting ended.

13 Fairley's Memo: the Time Management Survey

The first objective was to discover the percentage of managers unable to keep up to date with their work.

The first question in the survey sent to eighty-eight managers, including regional directors, was: *Are you able to keep up to date on a daily basis with your work load?*

The answers showed that forty-six of our managers did, most of the time, keep up to date with their work. However, thirty-five of these men and women added comments that on several occasions, due to problems arising – illness of staff, etc. – tasks had to be postponed, or taken home for completion.

From this it would seem that nearly half our management team were not aware of time management procedures, while others, in spite of this awareness, could not cope with the day's tasks on a number of occasions. This, obviously, showed the need for us to introduce time management courses as soon as possible.

Our second question sent to the same managers was to ask them for their views on what should be included in a time management course – time wasters as well as time saving objectives, applicable either to themselves or to others who might stop them from completing their tasks on time.

Managers were told not to mention colleagues' names when answering this question. There were the usual frivolous comments and statements which did not come within the scope of the survey. For example, managers complained of inefficient staff, non-co-operation from other managers, personal illness, etc.

After deleting such answers, and sieving out those which were repetitive, the following summarised the managers' comments (As expected most time management problems applied to others rather than to themselves):

* Mr A must waste hours looking for notes, papers, information. His office is cluttered up with old trade magazines, a collection of menus, plus copy correspondence. He says he can put his hand on anything required at a moment's notice. He can't!
* Too many demands from those above who *must* be given priority. You can't tell a managing director that you can't provide him with data required within the time set; you just get on with the job, and important routine work suffers. This goes right down to shop foreman and supervisor. The foreman makes demands of the supervisor: the works manager wants immediate action from the foreman . . . Investigations show that rarely is there any great urgency for the majority of these demands. It seems an executive habit to write on a memo *as soon as possible*. What is the use of introducing time management procedures when the problem starts at the top? If the top executives stopped making these demands it would go right down the line, and we should all be able to get our work done efficiently.
* I work to a set plan. I keep a diary, detailing the day's work. First I enter the set tasks – telephoning, correspondence, meetings, dictating. Then I make time for priority work, followed by routine tasks. In between, there's always time to spare – between appointments, or by taking a shorter lunch . . . These are the time fillers that I usually use for reading and checking. In our group I'm the only manager who keeps such a diary, and the only one who keeps up to date with his work, and doesn't

complain of overwork.

* Transfer Mr Y, and we'll all have time to spare! He's a compulsive talker. It doesn't matter how busy we are – and he can see that we're busy – he still insists on telling us in detail about his holiday, golfing experience, gardening; and it's always a minute by minute description. There is no stopping him, and unfortunately, there are many like him.

* Too much reading matter – too many memos – too many trade magazines – too many direct mail letters . . . They should be sorted through by someone – but not us!

* Too many interruptions.

* Too many meetings.

* Too much paper work. Mrs J has a very poor filing system and we all suffer from it.

* No one is ever willing to take our dictation, or tapes.

* Director K always complains of being behind with his work, but overlooks the fact that he is a 'committee man'. Whatever he is offered in the way of joining a group, trade association, local tennis club committee, Government sponsored body . . . he will accept. Consequently, at least twice a week he is out of his office, attending one of his meetings or lunches. There's nothing wrong with that, but he complains that he has to take work home.

* I discovered a major time waster in myself. I entertained too much! I always made myself believe that it was for the benefit of the company. It wasn't! It was for my benefit: I enjoyed it. This would have continued, but unfortunately I had some heart trouble and my doctor told me I had to stick to a rigid diet. Now I see the error of my ways. I was carrying out an enjoyable time wasting exercise. There are thousands like me in industry – many, presumably, like me, getting behind with their work.

These were the most frequently recurring time consuming points raised. We then listed them under precise headings, and asked our managers to place them in order of priority. These are the first two:

1 Time wasting activities by others usually affect our time management.
2 Not working to set priorities upsets our time management.

This surprised us. We had thought that 'not working to set priorities' would easily come first, with 'unnecessary paper work' second, and 'keeping a diary' third.

Obviously, we had got our priorities wrong!

Next, we carried out tests over a four-week period, at two different venues.

Class A: Eight managers who complained of never being able to keep up to date were our target.
Class B: Eight managers priding themselves on their systems – whether these were log diaries or a series of files – were our next target. These eight managers, in spite of their efficient systems, were still behind with their work.

We called a meeting of Class A and instructed them in sophisticated ways of improving time management. They were asked to keep a daily timed diary, to ensure that every minute was used efficiently. They were given action delay folders; they were asked to delegate more. We appointed a controller, to work closely with those managers.

We held a similar meeting with Class B and told them to continue with their good time management practices, but asked them to co-operate in an exercise to cut out time wasting. This, too, was under the supervision of a controller. We laid down the following rules for them: no open door policies; colleagues who attempted to talk about anything, other than business, were to be laughed out of court (naturally, this did not apply to out of office hours); no chatting up staff; telephone calls cut to a maximum of three minutes except, of course, for customer contacts. No meetings were to last longer than thirty minutes, unless permission had been given by the controller; no extraneous matters to conflict with time control – for example, time off for shopping or moving, late at the office for any reason, entertaining friends during office hours . . . Executives were instructed not to send urgent messages 'for action now' when no immediate action was required. Customers excepted, all appointments must be kept on time, otherwise the interviews should be cancelled. There must be no interruption to work, unless a crisis occurs (the controller to decide on whether or not it is a crisis). Cut down on the sending of memos.

Both exercises lasted four weeks. The result of this was that Class B cut out all time wasters and found they had time to spare, while Class A with all their skills and management procedures were still not quite up to date with their work, due to all the time wasting reasons given to Class B.

It is not generally realised how much time wasting goes on in offices – self generated, and generated by others. It could well average an hour a day or more.

The lesson, surely, is that we must be tougher on time wasters, because time management procedures themselves are not the complete answer.

Following this survey we offered a prize for the most succinct statement on time management practices. The winner was Max Lincoln, distribution/transport manager at Dorset. The pressure on his time was enormous. Every salesman/buyer demands quick delivery, or a rapid collection of parts without which the production manager claims that the production line will stop flowing. He is overloaded with paper work, while there is a continual problem of service engineers' vans breaking down.

In spite of all these problems, Lincoln maintains that he is able to keep up to date with his work, and he doesn't take work home.

Here is his winning entry (I am not giving the introduction, only the points Lincoln has emphasised):

1 Prove to top management that paper work can be cut by 50 per cent without any loss of efficiency. My advice was accepted. It's a pity the same exercise isn't carried out in other departments!

2 Every six months I keep a time log – for one week only. A permanent log, I have found, is of little use, because it is so disregarded. This six-monthly log covering one week of my time gives the exact details of use of telephone, dictation, checking, discussions, attending meetings, instructing, advising, socialising, delegating or not delegating, being interrupted . . .

   The log always comes as a shock, because it's so easy to fall into bad habits, but at least for some few months after keeping the log my time management improves, every time. That is why it is essential to have this six-monthly check.

3 Continually cut down report systems, especially those required from those delivering or servicing. If I don't use the information quickly I cut it out altogether, and no longer make a request for it.

4 Always tackle the unpleasant tasks quickly, otherwise too much time is taken up in thinking about them.

5 Always set priorities with the difficult tasks high on the list. But remember that most priorities are simply requests which someone else feels are urgent. I, therefore, decide what is urgent and what is not – and I will not be pressurised into giving priority to tasks which I know are not that urgent. Mostly, I take the day's work in an orderly fashion and only rarely do I admit that there is a top priority – although

obviously, some jobs are more urgent than others.

6   Having made my decision under (5) I do use action delay folders after I have decided what needs action that day, what can be delegated and what can be delayed without any adverse effect.

7   I make certain that all filing concerned with my department is up to date daily – and woe betide any of my staff who let me down in this respect!

8   When I go away I expect my work to be done by my assistant. I don't believe that 'holding the fort' is good enough. He has to do better than that. He has to think constructively as well as carry out routine tasks. My instructions are do it right or do it wrong – but leave nothing for me to decide when I return.

9   I never spend unnecessary time on work that I enjoy doing. This is a great managerial weakness and is a real time waster for many of my colleagues. I enjoy motoring, and could easily find a reason most weeks for driving to Wales, Scotland – or Land's End for that matter – and I could take my wife with me. But I have stopped misleading myself. I refuse to be motivated by what I enjoy doing, and I am only motivated by what is right from a business point of view.

10 I always set myself deadlines to complete a task.

11 Never take work home. I know for a fact that at least two managers take work home to impress their partners, or as an excuse for not being able to look after the children, or do housework – cunning! Good time management, to me, means completing the day's tasks within office hours. If this can't be done, then the reason must be discovered and it is possible that the back-up staff is wrong.

12 In spite of (11) all managers take home some creative work which should, also, be enjoyable work. I am not referring to worries, because worry is something more often encountered by the manager who doesn't feel capable of undertaking a task, or solving a

problem. I am referring to creativity which will improve the service we offer – which will enable me to deliver more speedily, to choose my cars more carefully, or even, as happened most recently, produce a brochure to show how our distribution works. These creative thoughts can occur at any time – while watching the television, or gardening . . . I don't believe anyone can sit down and say to himself, *now I'll think creatively*.

13 I am not a perfectionist. 90 per cent suits me; it's better to get a task complete and 90 per cent right than to waste my own and other people's time trying to achieve what is probably unachievable.

14 Although I do not allow other people to waste my time, I have all the time in the world for any of my staff who may have personal problems. I don't call this time wasting, it is building morale for the benefit of the company. If possible, however, I do try to discuss their problems with them out of office hours.

15 At every interview – for example, it might be a salesman calling to see me – I explain the time I have available, making a reasonable excuse for not being able to give more of my time.

16 I have become adept at *skip* reading – which means picking out the essential factors in newspapers, books, or magazines, and skipping the rest. *Skip* reading is quick to master, while *speed* reading is very, very rarely mastered.

17 I do not allow representatives to entertain me, and I don't entertain colleagues under the pretence of *it's the only time we can get together*.

18 A very efficient secretary enables me to save endless time.

19 I have a *filler* folder. In it I keep details of minor matters which it would be nice to settle that day – although not essential.

20 I avoid going to conferences where I know that I shall

only hear speakers reiterating what they have previously said and written about, time and time again. Too many managers attend conferences purely for their entertainment value, and to enable them to meet old friends.

21 I delegate.

22 When I hold a meeting I make sure the following points are adhered to:

Each meeting must have a clearly defined objective, and no discussion is allowed which is not relevant to that objective.

At nearly every meeting there is a compulsive talker and a silent listener. My job is to encourage the silent listener to express his opinions and to stop the compulsive talker from monopolising the meeting so that it runs overtime.

At the commencement of each meeting a time schedule is agreed: a time limit set for each point on the agenda, and a finishing time.

Minute-taking is kept to a minimum.

Attendance is restricted to those whose presence is essential. This saves wasting the time of people who may feel affronted because they have not been invited to attend.

We don't avoid taking immediate action by referring a matter to a sub-committee. Sub-committees rarely produce evidence. If a meeting is worth holding all relevant information should be available so as to enable decisions to be made.

The best time-saver of all is to cut meetings to a minimum. Ask these questions before deciding to hold a meeting: (a) what may we get out of this meeting that could not be achieved in other less time-consuming ways? and (b) am I quite sure I have not called it to air my own views and boost my own importance?

One very good test of executive efficiency is that *few* meetings are held.

End of Prize Winning Entry

You will all agree that Max Lincoln deserved to win, although there were many other excellent entries and some points were repeated.

Lincoln, in spite of his apparently strict régime, is noted for the fact that he is a great friend to have. He is always there in time of need, and he is looked up to for his fairness. He is a very loyal member of the staff and a most kindly person – just tough on time management, as well as other aspects.

All of you, with the possible exception of Don McAllister, know that during the last ten days Lincoln has been appointed regional director. One day he will be heading for the main board.

This memorandum has covered most of the main features of good time management. Tim Currie, who has written many articles on time management, suggested the following points should be included in it:

1   Time management is concerned with *planning* more than *doing*. If planning is meticulous everything else will fall into shape. There should be *planning* for time spent on organising and administration; *planning* for getting the best out of a time saving factor – for example, before using the telephone how many managers note down the points they want to raise during the conversation? This alone would turn a conversation into a much shortened but more effective business call.

2   If any department within an organisation is a weak link, this will result in a manager wasting time rectifying faults. Get the department right, and the time management will become right!

3   Develop procedures which will standardise much of the work – standard letters, standard forms, simplified reports, standard lectures, standard sentences for secretaries to save lengthy dictation . . .

4   Always leave time for emergencies during each day.
    Rarely a day passes for a manager unless there is some
    kind of an emergency, but if this should not occur,
    then there is another 'filler' time available.
5   Ask your secretary to arrive early and leave early. She
    can then organise the mail, disposing of direct mail
    letters which are not of interest to her manager,
    putting aside those letters which she can deal with
    herself, obtain information if this should be necessary
    before replies can be dictated.
6   Never cut down on files. It is better to have too many
    files than too few. That way, you can put your hand
    to anything at a moment's notice.

We are now preparing a time management course which
all managers will be asked to attend. Undoubtedly, a
manager who doesn't give the impression of being
continually overworked, i.e. who carries out time
management processes, doesn't take kindly to time
wasters, and doesn't waste other people's time himself, is
exemplifying motivating leadership.

                                              Hugh Fairley

14 The Right Way to Delegate

Contrary to rumours the Fairleys were a very happily married couple. The rumours had started when Liza seemed to be continually away from home, but she was a unique person, and it was her uniqueness which had attracted Hugh Fairley to her in the first place. She was a fine horsewoman, a near-champion skier, and a most adventurous traveller, having journeyed, among other places, to Tibet, and rafted down the Amazon. She was also a Miss World look-alike, with a figure that was more seductive than that of many a pin-up. On the other hand, Liza was not interested in children, had no dress sense to enhance her curvaceous body, and was a most untidy person.

They had bought an old, rambling manor house at Willsby in Buckinghamshire, with the intention of renovating it, but so far only his study had been redecorated and refurnished, although some money had also been spent on the paddock for their three horses.

On the day of the meeting Liza and Joy, the girl who helped with the horses, had tidied up the huge living room and, with a forecast of wintry showers, had lit a log fire which blazed away creating an 'olde worlde' atmosphere.

None of Fairley's colleagues had visited the manor house previously, but all had met Liza at various Huntley functions. When McAllister and the directors arrived, Liza, dressed in riding kit, met them, again impressing

them with her natural charm, but after a few minutes'
chat she said, "You don't want me hanging around, I'll
see you all later."

This met with a chorus proclaiming that they *would*
like to have her around, but she explained that she had
promised to help a friend at her riding stables. "But," she
added, "Joy will be here to organise coffee and lunch for
you." With that, she planted a long, lingering kiss on
Hugh and hurried away.

Fairley, being quite used to her unpredictable ways,
made no comment, but led the men into the living room
– a room overheated near the fireplace, and extremely
cold at the extremities. Although they had decided to
install central heating they had not yet got around to it,
and the house, therefore, was permanently cold.

Chairs had been arranged in a circle just out of range of
the direct heat of the fire, and when they were all
comfortably seated Fairley called on Don McAllister to
open the final session.

McAllister began with a question: *In view of Hugh's
time management memo, why don't managers delegate more
effectively?*

Manley said, "To my mind there are four kinds of
manager: the one who delegates for the wrong reason –
he dislikes doing a certain job; the one who delegates
because he can't do a certain job; the one who refuses to
delegate, because he believes that no one else can do the
job as well as he; and the fourth – the manager who likes
everyone to believe he is overworked."

"Excellent!" said McAllister. "Let's begin with the
manager who delegates because he dislikes undertaking
certain tasks."

"That covers seventy-five per cent of managers," said
Lawson. "They delegate not to save themselves time, but
to save being bored. There's nothing wrong with that if
the subordinate believes the task is important – for
example, telling a subordinate to read reports and then

submit a précis is good delegating. Both the subordinate and the manager profit. But tell a subordinate to carry out a similar task when that subordinate knows that the manager will hardly bother to glance at the précis and is just passing on a job he doesn't like doing himself – that's demotivating."

"He's not so bad," said Duckworth, "as the manager who, fearing failure, passes a task over to a subordinate. I'll give you an example – one of our sales managers, a man risen from the ranks of salesmen, instigated a campaign to sell extinguishers to professional people – especially accountants. He was a fine salesman but had no flair for writing copy or designing advertisements. Deciding to carry out a test campaign before submitting his ideas to the marketing director, he planned a direct mail shot and a small advertising campaign.

"He gave the job of supervising the publicity and direct mail advertising to a bright young accountant, in the belief that to sell to accountants he should seek the advice of an accountant and that an accountant would know what would appeal to his fellow professionals – that was his excuse, anyway. You remember the case, Tom, don't you?"

Tom nodded. "It was Bert Parkinson. He's no longer with us."

Duckworth continued, "Parkinson wasn't a creative person and, wishing to take all the credit instead of going to creative people, he delegated to the wrong person. My attention was drawn to the campaign when the regional managing director happened to see an advertisement in *Accountancy Weekly*, which he thought was dreadful and brought it to my notice.

"A good example, I think, of what can be termed incompetent delegating. I agree with Bill, too many managers who lack confidence in themselves delegate so that they have others to blame if things go wrong."

McAllister interrupted, "Before we continue let me

make a point: don't you think we're spending too much time on negatives – the reasons why managers delegate for the wrong reasons? Surely we're here to find the cures!"

"And that," said Hugh Fairley, "is the snag. If a managing director delegates for the wrong reasons, who is to correct him? If a manager is unable to tackle a task and passes it on to an inexperienced subordinate, who is to point out to him the error of his ways? How can these faults ever be discovered? All we can do is to pinpoint the fundamental errors, and ensure that they are given publicity at meetings, at our courses, in our house magazines and in books obtainable from our library. The only hope is that one day, a manager will see himself as others see him and delegate for the right reasons in the future.

"But how about Bill's other example – the manager who trusts no one and insists on doing everything himself? In my experience there are two reasons for this action – or non-action: one, that the manager wants to make himself indispensable. If no one knows how his daily tasks are accomplished, then the fear of losing out to a subordinate is lessened. The second reason is that the manager is speaking the truth and there *is* no one in his team able to carry out delegated tasks effectively."

Manley interrupted, "Which surely means that the manager himself is either choosing the wrong staff or has no staff training programme!"

"May I butt in?" asked Lawson.

"Certainly!"

"Many of the managers are not responsible for engaging their staff. Staff are forced on them by a director or a personnel manager. He can't sack anyone, and his superior may not take too kindly to any criticism of the interviewing and selection procedures."

"In that case," said Fairley, "the situation becomes impossible! However, I am sure that when managers give inadequate staff as a reason for not delegating, they are, mostly, making excuses for their own weaknesses.

"Only a tiny minority of a work force is untrainable. These are the difficult people who are against everything and everybody. But let us consider the majority of cases, when the manager only believes that a subordinate cannot do a task and there is no validity in his belief. What do we do about that?"

"Another brick wall," said Lawson. "There is nothing that can be done except by instruction from above."

Fairley answered, "I can only repeat, so much depends on us and the training we give. You may be sure that I shall have a meeting with our training managers. There will have to be more case studies and films produced on how to inspire a manager and show him how to delegate effectively. Putting it more simply: no training – no results."

McAllister said, "You are echoing the words my consultants use daily to their clients."

Fairley smiled, nodded his appreciation, then continued, "But what of the man who worries in case anyone should think he is not working every minute of his eight-hour day? A psychologist might tell us that if there is some psychological urge for someone to impress upon others the enormous work load he carries, it is probably good for him – if boring for others. This type of manager is, invariably, a moaner, always complaining of his overwork but refusing to delegate, to ease his burden. Training won't help him – he will rarely see anyone else's viewpoint, because he, in a strange way, enjoys his overwork. A friendly talk can, sometimes, work wonders – this man is probably starved of praise. He feels that others don't realise his importance, and that is why he has to prove his worth by over-working."

McAllister said, "What we all have to do now is to think for a few moments, and ask ourselves whether we come under any of Bill's four headings."

"I do," said Larry Duckworth. "I'm apt to believe in the old tag *by the time I've instructed someone else I can complete the task myself*. I know I'm wrong. I should overcome subordinates' weaknesses if they have any, so that they can all take over some of my work. I'll try to put that right in the future."

"Well spoken, Larry," said McAllister. "Now we'll consider another aspect of delegating: Does delegating build or lower morale?"

"Both," said Fairley. "It builds morale if a subordinate is given a task which it is within his capabilities to complete, makes him feel that he is trusted, and involved in senior management. It lowers morale if the task is one beyond his capabilities, or one in which, on completion, the manager seems to have lost interest. For example, when the Old Man asked me to take his place at a top level meeting with André Gervaise to discuss the taking over of his company in Lyons, and told me that he would respect my decisions, I was over the moon. It was a task well within my capabilities. When, however, he once asked me to read three technical books – and I'm not a technical man – and let him have a précis, my morale went right down. He had obviously realised at a glance that the books were padded and, possibly, boring, and he didn't want to be bothered. I thought at the time that the task should have been given to his own P.A., not me, so it lowered my morale. But only for a short time."

McAllister said, "A good example, Hugh. Too often we delegate tasks which don't give satisfaction to a subordinate. But there are many routine managerial tasks which are, perhaps, boring but have to be completed on time, nevertheless – and this can only be achieved by delegating."

"Of course," said Fairley, "but when giving such routine tasks, the reasons should be explained. A 'please help me' or 'I have a problem which you can help me solve', or 'I know you won't like this but knowing you

you'll do it well, just the same', can change a subordinate's outlook completely. It's all a question of
approach. What must not happen is for a subordinate to
say to a colleague, 'Look what he's lumbered me with
this time!' "

"I couldn't care less what a subordinate thinks, so long
as the work gets done," said Manley.

"Then you're wrong!"

"I don't think so. We can't question ourselves about
every action we take."

"I'm not suggesting that," said Fairley. "But there is a
right way and a wrong way of delegating. It hurts no
manager to do it the right way."

McAllister held up his hand. "You're both correct. We
are only human, and we can't, when under pressure,
always remember the niceties of life. But for all that,
thoughtfulness when delegating does make routine work
more acceptable.

"But surely we're discussing the delegating of more
important issues? May I remind you of our objective –
motivating leadership. We are, therefore, considering
delegating as a *motivating force* as well as one aspect of
time management. And there's no doubt, delegating can
be a considerable motivator."

"Obviously," said Lawson, "but unfortunately, we all
too often miss the obvious. When I was an assistant sales
manager I was asked by the sales manager to help him
out by designing a new sales leaflet. I was delighted!"

"But had you any flair for designing?" asked
McAllister.

"I had, because my sales manager, Danny Coles, had
sent me on a course which included innovation – which,
itself, included the preparation of sales literature and
advertising copy."

Bill Manley said, "Can't we save time and just say that
we should train subordinates to take on additional
tasks?"

"That *is* our policy," said Fairley, "but managers only pay lip service to such training. We have to nag them to send staff to our courses – the excuse is always that they are *too busy*. The real reason is often incompetence or laziness on the part of the manager."

"Or," said Lawson, "a fear that if the subordinate has greater knowledge of a subject than his manager, that might erode the manager's authority. Another point sometimes raised is that a subordinate, through acquiring extra knowledgc, may believe that he is worth more to the company and, therefore, ask for a salary increase."

McAllister said, "That point was raised earlier. In all my experience I have never known it to happen. It's an excuse for not giving training."

Fairley said, "It all boils down to what we keep repeating: that we on the main board should emphasise the need for both managers and subordinates to acquire greater knowledge and skills. First train the managers so that they can train the subordinates – or, equally important, we have to show staff how, by self development, they can achieve greater success."

"Let's leave the training of subordinates for a while," said Larry Duckworth. "There are other aspects of delegating that, so far, we have not touched on. The first is understanding our own limitations, and delegating tasks to others who are more competent to tackle them. For example, I'm not very good – in fact, I'm pretty bad – at writing articles for magazines, newspapers, etc., but I'm constantly being asked for such articles covering finance, accountancy, computers . . . for magazines and periodicals covering these subjects. I have Harold Lester in my department. He's a highly competent writer with a good command of language, so I always brief him to write the articles for me. This may be a bit like cheating, but I believe it's right because they want my name under the articles."

"You need not worry about that!" said McAllister.

"Politicians and sportsmen do it all the time. If it weren't for ghost-writers they would rarely see their names in print. But all too few managers look for this hidden talent. It is often they who complain that no one can do a job as well as they can themselves."

Lawson said, "The reason why so many managers know so little about their subordinates' abilities is that they do not appraise them. If they did, they might find talents which could be of great benefit to the company as well as to themselves. It also improves the relationship between manager and subordinate. I don't believe in six-monthly appraisals, but I do ask my team of managers to carry out regular appraisal exercises, although they don't always do as I ask."

"I agree," said Manley. "But there's one aspect of delegating which demotivates. I'm referring to the manager who always delegates the task he doesn't like to the subordinate he doesn't like, or alternatively, to one weak enough to accept commissions without demur."

Fairley said, "It still comes down to education. But a worse example of wrong delegation is the manager who delegates the unpleasant tasks – a reprimand, a dismissal, or demands from a customer which he knows cannot possibly be met. No manager worthy of the name should ever delegate the unpleasant tasks."

Duckworth said, "I don't think any of us can be accused of shirking any issues, however unpleasant."

"Of course not," said Manley. "But we mustn't forget that there are a helluva lot of managers who do – and we're here to try and do something about it. If we don't do something about it, these exercises are a waste of time!"

Fairley went on, "May I tie up the issue by giving you a series of answers to questions given to subordinates at a session on delegating at our courses? We wanted to get their point of view rather than the managers' viewpoint.

"The trainer wrote on the board, 'Why I fouled it up'.

He then explained to those present that what he wanted
to hear from them was why tasks delegated to them were
not completed satisfactorily. Here are some of the
answers!"

Fairley read from notes: " 'It wasn't made clear what I
had to do.' 'He gave me a list and said get on with it –
with what, I don't know!' 'Do some research, I was told.
Find out what the customer is thinking. How was I
supposed to go about that? Was I allowed to travel? Was
I allowed to claim any expenses? Was I to use the
telephone only? Was I to write – and if so, who was going
to type my letters?' "

Fairley stopped reading and said, "And there are more
in similar vein; but now, I'll continue with a different
kind of answer to the same question: 'I don't think he
knows what he wants.' 'Like Micawber, he hopes something will turn up from my investigation.' 'He doesn't
understand the working of the computer, so he expects
the impossible.' "

"And again, more in similar vein," Fairley
commented; "and here is another different set of
answers: 'I was ticked off for exceeding my authority', 'I
was given no guidance as to how much I could spend and
was then reprimanded for overspending', 'I didn't know
that I was not allowed to approach Mr X for
information.'

"And," said Fairley, "there are more additions to that
theme as well. But let me break away for a moment. It
seems that we shall not finish here until about six-thirty.
As this is the final session I hope you can all stay on for a
little celebration – the drinks are all lined up."

They all felt that celebrations were in order, and
agreed to stay for a while.

"That's settled then," said Fairley. "Now for some
rules which we told subordinates that managers would be
given in the future to ease the subordinates' burden,
when tasks were delegated to them.

"One, managers must explain precisely what has to be done, and if this is not clarified, subordinates are entitled to ask for clarification.

"Two, managers must know the exact objectives of the tasks, so that they can give proper guidance. If objectives are not clear, subordinates should ask for further information.

"Three, managers must tell subordinates the exact limits of their authority. Again, subordinates must ask for these limits if they are not given."

There followed discussions on the reasons given by subordinates for not being able to complete tasks, and the way the main board should apply itself in the future to ensuring that managers did delegate efficiently, and for the right reasons.

This was followed by a break for lunch. They were all a little surprised when lunch turned out to consist of beer and sandwiches, served by Joy.

When the meeting recommenced at two o'clock McAllister said, "What I should like to do now is to list some principles of delegating not already fully covered, to be followed by further discussions leading to action plans for the future. I shall be using the word *you* in its generic sense, to refer to managers generally.

Like Fairley before him, McAllister then read from notes:

"One, you should always monitor the progress of a task delegated, otherwise costly mistakes may be made. I'll tell you of one that was not costly, but was indicative of what could go wrong. We were called in by the managing director of a group employing two hundred salesmen. Our assignment was to seek ways of cutting sales costs. Here is an example of money wasted: the sales director had decided to send a bowl of flowers each month to the wife of the most successful salesman. He delegated the task of ordering and ensuring that the bowl was despatched on time to a young lady in his department. For something like three years, until our consultant was called in, each month the wife of one of the salesmen received a most expensive bowl of flowers – especially during out-of-season periods. He pointed out that the cost could have been reduced by a third without any demotivating effect. The ladies would have been just as delighted to receive a less expensive bowl. A simple case of a sales director delegating, but not monitoring, a task.

"The policy must be the same whether the task is small or of major importance. Lack of monitoring can be extremely costly."

Lawson interrupted, "I sometimes call that *delegating by not wanting to know*. There are many executives who would rather not be asked questions about costs. Then they are able to criticise over-expenditure on the part of subordinates. Sorry, Don, for interrupting you."

McAllister said nothing – smiled, and continued, "Two – and this cannot be over-emphasised, it is so important – the manager must make sure that the subordinate has the skill to complete the task. This really comes under the heading of *performance appraisal*.

"Three, a subordinate must never be allowed to sub-delegate a task, without permission.

"Four, beware of the over-enthusiastic subordinate, who always requests tasks but rarely completes them. We call this type a subordinate grasshopper – someone always looking for new challenges, but never achieving victories. The grasshopper always finds something else to engage his time and efforts which must receive priority. If pressed for completion, he can even take refuge in illness.

"Give tasks to enthusiasts, by all means, but make sure that they are not members of the grasshopping fraternity.

"Five, make resources available to the subordinate – not only money, but the right to take any appropriate action.

"Six, when a delegated task has been successfully completed, always give credit to the subordinate.

"Seven, if a task has not been satisfactorily concluded, investigate the reasons before apportioning blame. It could be that the failure is due to one of the many reasons already given as a cause of failure.

"Eight, ask yourself at regular intervals, *Why do I do this? Why do I do that?* The answer might be that you need not do 'this' or 'that', and a subordinate would be delighted to have the opportunity of taking over the task and thus acquiring greater authority.

"Nine, even if you can do a task better than a subordinate, you should allow the subordinate to take over such tasks now and again. Only in this way can he improve his skills and gain experience."

McAllister paused for a moment, then said, "Some of these nine points we have partly covered before, but they are worth discussing again."

Time passed quickly, with each of the directors proving a point by telling a personal story or anecdote.

Six-thirty arrived all too soon. Hugh Fairley said, "Drinks are being served in the dining-room. If you'll all return here in five minutes, I'll take you through to the bar." After ten minutes, Hugh led the way into the adjoining room.

The door opened. First, there was complete silence. Then whoops of joy, and later, hugging and kissing. In the room were Angela Duckworth, Susan McAllister, Debbie Lawson, Alice Manley and, of course, Liza Fairley.

Later, Fairley explained that the wives had been in the know for about a fortnight, and thus proved, once and for all, that wives could keep secrets – possibly better than their husbands.

"I thought a surprise dinner party would be just right for this evening," Liza Fairley said. She had arranged for the catering to be taken over by two excellent cooks who needed the additional income, having just opened a local restaurant.

The first course was duck pâté and truffles, and with it went a 1979 Pouilly Fumé. The main course, served to each guest on a plate protected by a silver cover, was baked fillet of lamb cooked in pastry, with green parsley sauce. The vegetables were soufflé potatoes and french beans; the wine was an outstanding 1971 first-growth Château Latour, which, Hugh explained, he had been saving for just such a celebration. The sweet – Marchise au chocolat – a very light chocolate cream served in a chocolate case, they all agreed, provided an ideal finish to a perfect dinner.

After the meal Tom Lawson gave the loyal toast, and this was followed by McAllister, with a toast to the ladies. Then Hugh Fairley stood up and said, "Tim Currie told us to try to keep after-dinner speeches below the five minute mark. I'm going to be even shorter than that. We have, I believe, achieved our objective, and are better motivating leaders today than we were eight months ago. A special thank you, therefore, to you, Don, for making it all possible. Will you all stand and join me in drinking a toast to Don McAllister, whose patience, charm, and counselling have been of such great help to us."

The glasses were raised in a final toast.

15   The Decision

It was 11 am when McAllister entered Roland Huntley's office. The chief executive was seated in his armchair, and by his side on a small table stood an ice bucket peeping from the top of which was the neck of a champagne bottle; alongside were two tulip-shaped glasses.

The men shook hands, and Huntley beckoned his visitor to a chair. "I've read your report," he said, "or to say I've skipped through it would be more truthful. It's packed with charts, graphs, grids, calculations, and every conceivable type of padding. The complete report could have been condensed into about five pages for each main issue, and you've given me three hundred and eighty pages."

McAllister said, "If we'd given you a condensed version you wouldn't have thought you'd had your money's worth. But you must have been pleased that we found so little in production, marketing, finance, or general strategy to criticise. For all that, the new systems we have suggested will, if carried out, save our fees for you ten times over."

"That being so," Huntley said, smiling, "let's celebrate! Will you open the bottle, Don – champagne corks always fight back when I try to extract them."

The glasses filled, Huntley said, "You have done a good job, Don, but there's bound to be criticism at the meeting next week-end, when you will face our regional directors and managers."

"I'm looking forward to that!"

Huntley nodded. He continued, "Your leadership seminars with my co-directors have ended, and the general view is that the objectives were achieved – a result to be expected. So let's drink to that."

Their glasses were raised.

Huntley said, "Now for the most important issue. Who is going to run the company in the future?" He paused, then went on abruptly, "Give me your views on my colleagues."

McAllister was too wise to be rushed into any quick comment. He drank some wine reflectively, then said, "It would be unfair of me to give verdicts gleaned from half a dozen or so meetings with men of the calibre of Manley, Lawson, Duckworth and Fairley. How can I add to the knowledge which you have already acquired through working with them for many years?"

Huntley said, "You're a perceptive person, Don. You can quickly see through the disguises, the acts, the pretences of men trying to impress you – and my friends, undoubtedly, went out of their way to do just that! You don't need years to form judgements; give me the personal opinions you formed while working with them."

"Very well. But my opinions shouldn't affect your judgement, although they may verify your own conclusions."

"That's all I'm looking for from you," said Huntley, topping up the glasses as both men relaxed.

McAllister said, "I'll begin with Bill Manley. He is an outstandingly good director of production, faced with the formidable task of overseeing not only the factories in this country, but the outposts of Huntley's overseas. He's a clear thinker, and knows how to get the best out of people. His directness may not always line up with Fairley's concept of human relations, but his subordinates understand him, and respect him. There can be few better production men in the country. These are the pluses.

"As against that, if he became chief executive he would not be the ideal negotiator with men of your calibre, Roland. He is too dogmatic. He will also always veer towards production at the possible expense of marketing. He is so emotionally involved in production that he may not take kindly to outside criticism and may dig his heels in for the wrong reasons.

"The main question facing all companies of your size is future strategy. Without planned strategy even the finest organisation can fall into a rut. We can think of a number of companies built by entrepreneurs like you which have failed under lesser men. In my opinion, if you are looking for a 'status quo' for the next few years, Manley will cope – and cope well. But if you are thinking of long-term strategy – say ten years – then you will have to evaluate his strengths and weaknesses as you know them, and decide whether you think he is the right man to plan ahead."

Huntley made no comment, but nodded his head.

"Now for Larry Duckworth," said McAllister. "On the face of it he has everything you can possibly require in a chief executive. He has a fine financial brain, and without that asset a chief executive can make many mistakes. Duckworth rules the budgets and forecasts with an iron rod. He also gives you excellent advice on capital expenditure and investment, is an extremely good administrator, and will always use the resources of the Huntley Group to good advantage. If an offer is made to take over another company, the other side will not mislead him by stock manipulation, profit manoeuvring, or unsubstantiated claims for the future. Also, he is respected by everyone for his clear thinking and his integrity."

"That seems almost good enough," said Huntley, "except that you must have a but –"

"Here's the but," went on McAllister. "Your success has been built on outstanding marketing and dynamic selling, and Duckworth is not a marketing man. Also, he is the type who could become a very remote figure, rarely seen by his subordinates. During the recession you increased marketing expenditure and cut in every other direction. I believe Duckworth, if he had been in command, would have done the reverse. If you were to appoint him your successor he would have to have a marketing director prepared to fight him every inch of the way. Would Tom Lawson do that? That, Roland, is for you to judge.

"The third, Tom Lawson, is, I think your favourite, because Tom has played such a big part in the growth of Huntley's – almost more than anyone else excepting you. Everyone likes Tom – all the managers work well with him. As a marketing sales promotion man he cannot be faulted. He is a top level negotiator and motivator, with a charming wife who believes it is his destiny to become chief of Huntley's. And there you have the pros.

"Now for the cons. He is not always rational in his thinking and can make the one big mistake which could cause a major setback to the Group. He is the type of executive who could put his own enjoyments, needs, and pleasures before the needs of the company – result, wasted money. To him, luxuries become necessities. You must ask yourself, is that the right example for a chief executive to set? He may well improve with greater authority – that often happens. But again, this is for you to judge.

"And finally, there is the obvious choice – Hugh Fairley. He has a fine personality and an adoring wife who would never make demands on him which could affect the company. If Hugh says it's right for Huntley's, then it's right for her!"

"Because of his experience when negotiating with trade union officials and your own managers he is able to handle almost any situation involving people. As a believer in human relations he would look after the welfare of every single person in the group – and that breeds loyalty. He has been involved in training so long that he has a good all-round knowledge of every aspect of management and marketing as well as finance and accountancy. Fairley will always be willing to listen to advice and never stubborn if, on facts presented to him, he believes his judgement to be wrong. He always wants to hear both sides of every argument."

"So you're making your choice," said Huntley.

"No, I'm not making any choice – that is for you. Now let's consider Fairley's possible weaknesses. Is he too nice? Is he strong enough to weather the bitter in-fighting that goes on in most companies? Can he stand the strains which you have had to accept – the constant demands which all become part of the business life of a chief executive?

"I'm not suggesting that he is a weak character, but I am suggesting that there is such a thing as being too kindly. Unfortunately, at times, a chief executive does have to act unfairly – does act irrationally – does upset people . . . and for the right reasons. Is Fairley tough enough to make these difficult decisions? I don't know! You know him better than I do. What I will say is that you, Roland, have had to be mighty tough to build this business, and whoever takes over from you has to have similar strengths to your own.

"Those, then, are my views – and remember, they are not in-depth views."

The men sipped their wine silently for a few minutes, then Huntley said, "Thank you, Don. As expected, you've hit the nail on the head, every time. Your judgements are all correct."

"What, then, is your decision – or is it wrong for me to ask?"

"No, you are within your rights to ask. The decision is

made difficult because none of my associates stands head
and shoulders above the others. Your views proved that.

"For this reason I have never named a successor, or
even appointed a deputy. I have not allowed anyone to
act totally for me in my absence. Is that a weakness, or a
strength?"

He paused, and McAllister said, "Surely there are only
two reasons for your action – or lack of action is, perhaps,
more apt. The first is that you didn't consider any of your
directors fit to take over. The second, that you like the
idea of four men jockeying for position – each trying to
outdo the others to impress you, and by those actions
carrying out their duties to even better purpose."

"Your conclusions are nearly right," said Huntley,
"but not quite. I have never considered the second
alternative of my friends jockeying for the position. But
there is a third aspect – that as they are all so good, it is
difficult to make a choice. Over the years each of them
has impressed me in turn.

McAllister said, "But you have to make some decision,
surely? How about bringing in someone from outside? I
could head hunt for you, you would then know who is in
the market for such a job."

Huntley shook his head. "That wouldn't work out.
How long does even a managing director last when a
company is taken over? Usually, he is out within six
months. If we brought in an outsider as chief executive
he would soon be confronted by Bill Manley with his
outspoken and direct manner – and then the new broom
would begin to sweep and out would go Bill. Every chief
executive introduced to a new company also has his own
pet associates, and he may well believe that he knows of a
marketing director who is better than Tom Lawson.
There would be upheavals, and tremendous changes, I
believe to the detriment of the company. I will not,
therefore, bring in anyone from outside. I know my team
is outstanding, and much too good to break up – you've

proved that in your report." He tapped the cover of McAllister's three hundred and eighty page report.

Huntley went on, "You've found weaknesses, and you have renewed their enthusiasm to improve their leadership qualities."

"Then who is it going to be?" asked McAllister. "Knowing you, you made up your mind long before this meeting."

"You're quite right," said Huntley. "I have made up my mind. But first, tell me, what would be *your* decision?"